Train Your Brain
for Success

A Teenager's Guide to Executive Functions

Randy Kulman, Ph.D.

Specialty Press, Inc.
300 N.W. 70th Ave., Suite 102
Plantation, Florida 33317

Cover Design: Michael Wall, Kall Graphics
Layout: Babs Kall, Kall Graphics

Illustrations by Peter J. Welleman

Specialty Press, Inc.
300 Northwest 70th Avenue, Suite 102
Plantation, Florida 33317
(954) 792-8100 • (800) 233-9273

Printed in the United States of America

ISBN-13: 978-1-886941762

ISBN-10: 1-886941-76-9

Library of Congress Cataloging-in-Publication Data

Kulman, Randy, 1955-

Train your brain for success : a teenager's guide to executive functions / by Randy Kulman.

   p. cm.

ISBN 978-1-886941-76-2 (alk. paper)

1. Learning, Psychology of–Juvenile literature. 2. Human information processing–Juvenile literature. 3. Brain–Localization of functions–Juvenile literature. I. Title.

LB1060.K855 2011

370.15'23–dc23

2011031730

Acknowledgments

Writing this book has been an opportunity to use what I have learned from the thousands of children and families with whom I have worked, as well as my own experience as a dad. Each of these individuals has helped to shape the issues and interests that are described in this book. I want to express my appreciation to my patients, students, family, and friends who have helped me in learning new things every day.

I would like to acknowledge the work of Peg Dawson and Richard Guare, who have translated theories of executive functioning into understandable skills that can be readily improved. I also thank my colleague and friend Gary Stoner for helping us to develop a research program that is leading to a better understanding of how to improve executive functions in children.

I am grateful to my staff at LearningWorks for Kids, James Daley, Philip Bishop, Patrick Elliot, Jennifer Slater, Pat Mullaney, and Stefanie Metko, for all of their ideas and help in editing this book. I also thank Deborah Swauger for her efforts at editing and keeping me on track and organized as I wrote this book.

Thanks are also owed to Harvey Parker at Specialty Press for believing in this project and being a great source of encouragement throughout the process. I appreciate the efforts of Peter Wellman at creating our illustrations and his willingness to make changes as necessary and of Babs Kall and Mike Wall from Kall Graphics for their creativity.

Most of all, I thank my family and friends for the support and knowledge that they have given me. My recently-deceased father Lawrence Kulman and my mother Clarissa Kulman provided assistance and were very "practical" when it came to making suggestions and have always set an example for me in caring about other people. I thank my dear friend Bill Sopp for his guidance and support in this book and my other ventures. I thank my partner Gail for her love, understanding and support in this and the dozens of other projects in which I find myself involved. I appreciate the opportunities that some really important kids in my life, Spencer, Maxwell, Madison, Gabriel, and Lauren, have given me in learning more about executive functioning in teenagers. Most of all, thank you to my children Scott, Seth, and Ethan, who are my greatest source of happiness and learning, for teaching me how to talk (or how not to talk) to teenagers. Hopefully I have learned a few things from you guys.

Table of Contents

1 Introduction – *How to Get Your Act Together* 1

2 Learning about Your Skills – *Take a Survey about Your Skills* 5

3 Organization – *Where is My Stuff?* 15

4 Planning – *What Should I Do?* 23

5 Focus – *When You Have to Pay Attention* 31

6 Time Management – *When You've Got Too Much to Do* 39

7 Self-control – *How to Stop, Relax, and Decide* 47

8 Flexibility – *Try Something New* 53

9 Working Memory – *If I Could Only Remember* 59

10 Self-awareness – *I Understand, I Understand* 67

11 High-tech Ways to Improve Your Skills – *Mom, Dad, I Need My Cell Phone!* . . 73

12 Keep on Going and Growing – *You Will Get Better and Better* 79

Addendum: Parents' Guide 81

Chapter 1
Introduction

How to Get Your Act Together

Sometimes it's just hard to get your act together. You have too many things to do, not enough time to do them, and you don't always know exactly where to begin. It becomes even harder to get it together when you can't find what you're looking for, your little brother or sister is annoying you, or you know that you're not remembering something that's really important.

It was tough enough when your elementary school teacher gave you a lot of homework. But once you get to middle school and high school, you've got five, six, or sometimes even eight teachers all giving you different types of work that is due on different days. And all of them have different expectations about how you should do it. If you're like a lot of kids, you're probably busy after school, as well. Maybe you're on a sports team or in a club, have an after-school job, or need to go home to get your brother or sister off the school bus.

Managing all this stuff is not easy. Lots of capable, smart, and hard-working kids feel that they're not doing everything as well as they should. Some of them are very forgetful and can't remember their homework. Others are so disorganized that they can't find it even when they do finish it all. Lots of kids have problems staying focused and paying attention, and others just aren't able to sustain their energy and effort enough to complete their work from start to finish.

Guess what? If you feel like this, you are not alone. Like many kids with these difficulties, you might just need to know that there is a reason for these problems that have become a part of your daily life. There is a very good chance that you need some help improving your executive functions. This book explains what executive functions are and shows you some really easy ways to improve these skills.

What Are Executive Functions?

Executive functions are a set of thinking, problem-solving, and self-control skills. Scientists who study the brain believe that they are situated in the most modern part of our brain, the prefrontal cortex, and that they connect to many other areas of our brain, as well. Some people refer to executive functions as being like the conductor of an orchestra. Just as an orchestra conductor decides what music to play and then directs, coordinates, and organizes the musicians to play it well, executive functions tell our brains what to do.

Executive functions help us to decide what to pay attention to in our lives. They may help us in planning and organizing our thoughts and activities and are useful in helping us to know how to get started on something and then how to manage our time. They also help us to control our behaviors and emotions and stop us from doing something thoughtless or something that might hurt ourselves.

As you can imagine, executive functions are very important to your success at school. They help you to pay attention in class and to understand and balance the material you are learning. They also help you to choose your behavior for different settings and to know how your actions will affect other people.

Some kids have more difficulties with their executive functions than others. These kids often report getting easily distracted at school, having problems starting and finishing their homework, and having difficulty remembering directions or what they have read. Fortunately, scientists who study the brain have begun to prove that learning new skills actually changes our brains, so that by practicing brain-based skills such as executive functions we can actually change the way our brains look and operate.

How to Use This Book

This book is organized around eight different sets of skills that capture the ways that kids use executive functions in school, at home, and in their other activities. At the end of each chapter are some very practical ideas for how you can improve your skills. The next-to-last chapter tells you about some really cool ways that you can use digital technologies such as cell phones, iPods, and the Internet to improve your self-management skills.

This is the kind of book where you don't have to read every chapter but can choose to skip around and look at the chapters that interest you most. To get the most out of this book, start by filling out and scoring the questionnaires in Chapter 2. These will give you a better idea of your particular strengths and weaknesses and help you to decide which areas you want to improve.

Please Read This

This is not a children's book. It is written for older kids who are capable of understanding their own strengths and weaknesses and who want to improve their skills.

The book is based on a few straightforward and simple ideas:

1. If you take the lead or choose to be an active partner in setting goals for yourself rather than having your teachers or parents set goals for you, you are more likely to improve in your area of choice.

2. If you believe that you can improve yourself and you work at it, you will do it. This is known as having a growth mindset, which is a way of saying that you know your willingness to improve and your efforts to keep working towards improvement will lead to improvement.

3. Unlike some personal characteristics, skills are not preset. For example, if you have stopped growing and you are 5' 6" tall, you will not be able to stretch yourself to 6' to help with your basketball abilities. On the other hand, you can improve your *skills* for running faster and jumping higher and, in turn, improve your game.

4. Skills require practice. By practice we don't mean just learning how to do them better, we mean the practice of *doing* them regularly. For example, if you learn how to do a tiring and complex dance routine or athletic activity very well and then stop practicing it for a while; you simply won't be as good at it.

5. The more you practice a skill the more it becomes a part of you. It's like when you brush your teeth (we hope you do it regularly). You probably aren't thinking too much about the pattern of your tooth brushing, but it is pretty much the same every time you brush.

Chapter 2
Learn About Your Executive Skills

Take a Survey About Your Skills

If you're like most kids you are probably good at some things and not as good at others. This is true about your executive functioning skills, as well. While every once in a while you might meet someone who seems to be good at everything, when you really look at other people you'll see that most of them have their own sets of strengths and weaknesses. Some people seem to be really good at a lot of things, but that might be because they choose to do the things that they are good at and enjoy.

Kids who are particularly good at reading, writing, and other subjects at school probably do well at them in part because they like them, the work comes easily to them, and they are areas that make them feel good about themselves. Kids who are really good at sports, art, or mechanics are probably good at them because they keep their interest and they keep practicing to get better at them. Those who like to hang out with their friends or who are always involved in group activities probably have good "people" skills or a lot of energy.

We encourage you to be careful not to compare yourself too much to other people. It's tough enough if you have a brother or sister who is noticeably better at a certain executive functioning skill than you are, such as paying attention or organization. However, you can probably think of some strengths that you have that your sibling does not have. More importantly, we encourage you to step back and look at the activities that you really like to do because you are likely to find that the executive-functioning skills that cause you so much trouble in school are not such a big deal during fun activities.

Now, wait a minute. That doesn't mean that you don't have to work on improving those executive-functioning skills for school. But if you notice that it's easier for you to pay attention and to start and finish an art project, build a birdhouse, or fix your bike than it is to study for a history test, then you've just learned something important about yourself.

We think about the things that truly interest and engage us as "lighting up your brain." When your brain is lit up, it tells you that there is more blood flow going to the parts of your brain (often the prefrontal cortex) where most of your executive-functioning skills come from and that they are working more efficiently for you. While neuroscientists are still studying how and why those parts of your brain light up when you are engaged in a task that you find interesting, they are starting to believe that it may have something to do with the reward centers in the brain, meaning that certain types of activities are more rewarding and stimulating for you.

Keep this information in the back of your mind; it will be important for you when you're older and have more of a choice about what you want to study, what field you want to work in, and what skill sets you want to improve. If you can involve yourself in activities that "light up your brain," everything else will work better for you. You'll probably be happier, get more accomplished, and feel better about yourself.

In the meantime, many kids who are reading this book will find that their brains do not "light up" as much as they'd like them to in school or when they are asked to do chores or other activities that they don't enjoy. As much as we would like to tell you not to worry about this or that when you are an adult you won't have to do anything that you don't want to do, that's not the case. So it makes a lot of sense to figure out strategies to get better at some of the executive functions that are difficult for you. Luckily we know that if you can identify the skills that you need to develop and then learn to practice them regularly, you will be able to improve these skills. Getting better at them might make something that wasn't of interest to you before "light up your brain" now.

How do you know if you are really struggling with executive functions? Some kids may not be aware of these difficulties at all. For example, if you are slow at finishing your work, you might think, "That's just the way I am." Other kids have problems with being focused and sustaining their attention. Many of these kids say that they have never been able to sit still for very long except for doing things such as playing video games, building with Legos or blocks, or watching a movie. Other executive-functioning difficulties may have developed over time and may not be quite as easy to see. For example, difficulty with planning probably didn't mean very much to you when you were younger because your parents and teachers planned everything for you. However, now that you are a teenager, you have a lot more activities and responsibilities for which you need to plan.

It would be unusual to hear a person with difficulties with executive functions say, "Oh, I've got a problem with organization," or "I have difficulty with my working memory." What you are more likely to notice is a feeling of frustration when you can't find your homework because it is somewhere, but you don't know where or when you are trying hard to remember all of the things that your mother asked you to do but you've got a nagging feeling that you've forgotten one or two of them. For teens, recognizing that you have difficulty with executive functions usually occurs because you are feeling discouraged, not doing as well as you want to do at something, taking longer than your friends to finish your work, or can't pay attention even when you are trying your hardest to do so.

Parents and teachers tend to see these weaknesses from another point of view. In fact, parents and teachers often begin to identify problems that kids have with executive functions when they are in their early elementary school years, but sometimes don't quite know how to label these difficulties. For example, your teacher might have said, "Jacob's desk is a complete mess. He can never find his pencil to start his work," or "Hannah talks so much in class that she is not paying attention to directions." When you get into your teen years, your parents are likely to say things such as, "If I don't sit with him to do his homework, he won't get it done," or "She's getting so moody and irritable, and acts upset about little things." Your teachers in middle school and high school might observe you and think that you don't care about your work or that you're just being lazy and taking too long to do your schoolwork. Unfortunately for kids who have difficulty with executive functioning, this type of negativity or lack of understanding can stick with you and influence your self-esteem.

The goal of this book is to help you figure out which of the executive functions you might want to improve. Most teenagers, even those who do really well in school and seem so organized and together, are likely to struggle in one or more of these areas. Kids who tell us that they have trouble with executive functions often have difficulty in several of these areas. In part, that's because they are related to each other. For example, kids who have problems planning out the steps needed to clean their room might also have problems organizing their belongings so that they know where things are.

Completing the following questionnaire will help you to understand if you have a particular difficulty with an executive function and how it might affect you at home, at school, or with your friends. Later in the book we list some fun and practical ways for you to practice and improve that executive function.

If you are ready, turn the page and answer each question as honestly as you can. Remember, the purpose of filling this out is to learn more about yourself so that you can work on improving. After you have completed the questionnaire, we will show you a bit more about your executive-functioning strengths and weaknesses. We also encourage you to complete a checklist at the end of the chapter that will help you to identify your strengths, as well as situations where the weaknesses that we just discovered may, in fact, be more of a strength.

Executive Functions Questionnaire

Please answer the following sentences as either true (by circling **T**) or false (by circling **F**). You will notice that many of these sentences use words such as often, easily, or regularly. This is because many of these sentences describe common difficulties for teens that can become problems when they occur again and again. Answer honestly so that you can better determine which of these areas may be a problem for you.

1

T/F   I often lose my stuff.

T/F   My backpack and bedroom are often messy.

T/F   My schoolwork, bedroom, or possessions are often disorganized.

2

T/F   I often find it hard to set long-term goals for myself.

T/F   I often do not plan how I am going to get things done such as homework, chores, or other activities.

T/F   I often do things randomly rather than take time to actively plan them step by step.

3

T/F   I am often easily distracted.

T/F   It is often hard for me to get started on things that do not interest me.

T/F   It is often hard for me to stay focused and pay attention to things that I do not enjoy.

4

T/F   I am often late to activities.

T/F   I often do not leave myself enough time to complete tasks even though I thought I had.

T/F   Often, I am not good at guessing how long homework or a chore will take.

5

T/F   I am easily frustrated.

T/F   I often act too quickly without thinking about the consequences of my behavior.

T/F   I can often become moody.

6

T/F   I often feel stuck because I like to do things a certain way.

T/F   I am often easily upset when someone changes my plans or an activity.

T/F   I often do not like new things.

7

T/F   I often find it difficult to follow many directions at one time.

T/F   I often find it difficult to do complex math problems in my head.

T/F   I often have trouble taking notes in school because I forget what was said.

8

T/F   I often find it difficult to explain why I have done something.

T/F   I often have trouble recognizing what other people are feeling.

T/F   I often have difficulty understanding and expressing my feelings.

Now that you have completed the questionnaire, it is very easy to score it. If you notice, the questions are separated into groups of three. If you answered true to all three in a group, this is an executive skill that you will want to address. If you circled two in the group, you also might want to consider working on that skill. If you have a score of 0 you have identified one of your executive function strengths.

Look below to see the skill to which each set of three questions refers and put your as either 0 if you stated **F** to all three questions or 1, 2, or 3, depending on how many **T**s you answered for each question.

_____ **1**   Organization

_____ **2**   Planning

_____ **3**   Focus

_____ **4**   Time management

_____ **5**   Self-control

_____ **6**   Flexibility

_____ **7**   Memory

_____ **8**   Self-awareness

We want you to understand that what you've just done is a rough estimate of your own executive-functioning skills. To know more about them, it would be helpful to have your parents fill out a set of similar questionnaires. To know even more, you could take a set of neuropsychological tests that provide even better information about your executive-functioning skills. What you are doing here, though, can serve as an excellent guide for helping you to determine your executive-functioning strengths and weaknesses. In particular, it helps to understand those areas that you see as an area of weakness that would be best for you to improve.

To get a first glimpse into what your scores mean, look at the following section. This will give you a very brief definition of each executive skill.

Experts and Students at Using Executive Functions

Now that you've scored your questionnaire, we encourage you to look at the executive functions for which you received your highest scores and those for which you received your lowest scores. Keep in mind that *a high score means that this is an area that you need to improve. A low score indicates that this is an area of strength for you.*

We have chosen to call people who have a great deal of knowledge about using a particular executive function and experience applying it in most situations "experts." We refer to someone with less mastery, who will also be likely to have difficulty applying a weaker executive function in new situations, a "student."

Before you go any further, we want to remind you of one of our most important themes. You can improve your skills through effort, a willingness to keep working on them, and a belief that your practice will lead to improvement. Even an expert needs to practice an executive function in order to maintain the skill. Perhaps more importantly, if you are a student and want to get better, you'll need to get training, learn from others, and keep practicing.

The charts here show what it means to be an Expert or a Student at Executive Functions.

Executive Function	Experts *are good at…*	Students *need help with…*
Organization	• Keeping track of their homework and assignments • Having a regular place to keep their cell phone, iPod, and other important personal items • Keeping track of their money	• Finding items in their backpack or room • Organizing their thoughts when writing an essay or book report • Keeping their locker or room clean

Executive Function	Experts *are good at...*	Students *need help with...*
Planning	• Setting long-term personal goals for themselves • Doing things with a system or order in place • Anticipating obstacles or delays that might disrupt their plans	• Thinking about future plans • Keeping track of multiple responsibilities at the same time • Planning time for activities, schoolwork, and chores so that they are able to complete them all
Focus	• Sustaining their attention to tasks or activities that are boring • Knowing how and where to get started on homework, projects, or chores • Keeping up their effort and attention in order to complete tasks	• Tuning out distractions and paying attention in class and at home • Learning how to get back on task if they get off track • Finishing a project before moving on to something else
Time Management	• Estimating how long it will take them to do something • Judging the difficulty of a task • Managing their time so they can get their work done and have fun	• Understanding the time it will take to do a large classroom project • Completing their schoolwork efficiently • Getting ready for school in the morning or other activities that have a specific start time
Self-Control	• Controlling their behavior when they get upset • Staying calm under pressure • Thinking before doing	• Slowing down to read directions before starting an activity • Handling frustration and anger • Taking their time to do homework and chores properly
Flexibility	• Trying out new activities • Adapting to changes in routine • Quickly recognizing when they are doing something wrong and correcting it	• Improving from mistakes • Being creative in problem solving • Learning how to deal with disappointments such as losing in a game or not getting picked for something
Working Memory	• Remembering and completing multi-step problems • Multitasking without being forgetful • Remembering what they have read	• Remembering where they put things such as their cell phone, keys, or homework • Following complicated directions • Listening and taking notes at the same time

Executive Function	Experts *are good at...*	Students *need help with...*
Self-Awareness	• Seeing things from another person's point of view • Understanding their strengths and weaknesses • Expressing themselves to others	• Understanding their strengths and weaknesses • Being aware of another person's reactions • Asking for help when they need it

Rate Your Strengths and Interests

If you are like most kids who are reading this book, you have probably found a few areas where you rated yourself as a "student" in regard to your executive-functioning skills. Being a "student" means that you have not had the opportunity or training to become an "expert" or that these skills may be harder for you to learn.

Early in the chapter we mentioned that activities that interest you are likely to "light up your brain" and help you to use your executive functions in the best way. When you are involved and doing the things that you love, your brain is far more likely to operate at peak efficiency. It is in these areas where you can become an "expert." We don't necessarily mean that if your brain "lights up" when you are playing videogames or cheering that you should plan on being a professional videogame player or cheerleader. We mean that these are activities in which you view yourself as working to your highest potential. We encourage you to think about what those strengths, interests, and activities are and how these characteristics contribute to who you are as a person. Doing so will help you to recognize and improve areas of executive-functioning weakness.

Look at the following lists of characteristics and areas of strength and interest. Check off *at least four* but *no more than eight* items from EACH of these lists that describe your most important characteristics/traits and interests/strengths/skills.

Characteristics/Traits

_____ Adaptability (I will try new things.)

_____ Affectionate (I love my friends and family.)

_____ Assertiveness (I can stick up for myself.)

_____ Cleanliness (I like things clean and neat.)

_____ Compassion (I care about other people and those in need.)

_____ Cooperation (I am a good team player.)

_____ Courtesy (I am very polite.)

___ Curiosity (I want to know more about everything.)

___ Dependability (People can count on me.)

___ Empathy (I understand what my friends are going through.)

___ Friendliness (I am upbeat and reach out to others.)

___ Honesty (I don't lie; I tell the truth.)

___ Humor (Most people think that I am very funny.)

___ Independence (I can make decisions and do things on my own.)

___ Motivation (I have the drive to get things done.)

___ Open-mindedness (I am open to learning new things and can accept criticism.)

___ Organization (I know where things are.)

___ Perseverance (I am a hard worker.)

___ Respectfulness (I am considerate of others' roles and needs.)

___ Responsibility (I can be counted on.)

___ Self-reliance (I can do many things on my own.)

Interests/Strengths/Skills

___ Art (e.g., draws, paints, makes pottery, takes photographs)

___ Animals (cares for animals and pets)

___ Carpentry (enjoys building things)

___ Collector (e.g., antiques, cards, other items)

___ Computers/Electronics (e.g., videogames, gaming online)

___ Current Events (e.g., watches the news, interested in history)

___ Dance (e.g., freestyle, jazz, modern dance)

___ Drama/Theater (acts or helps out in plays)

___ Fashion (e.g., style, design, sewing)

___ Individual Sports (e.g., running, tennis, gymnastics)

___ Mechanics (e.g., works with engines, cars, bikes)

___ Music (listens to or plays music)

___ Nature (e.g., being outdoors, camping, hiking)

___ Politics (is interested in government, politicians)

___ Popular Culture (is interested in celebrities, actors, or athletes)

___ Reading (reads on one's own)

___ Science (e.g., astronomy, biology, chemistry)

___ Spirituality (interested in religion, attends services)

___ Team Sports (e.g., soccer, basketball, softball/baseball)

___ Working (has a job; earns money)

___ Writing (e.g., stories, blogs, essays)

Now go back and take a look at the areas where you have weaknesses on the thinking skills survey. What you will probably notice is that you are better able to apply even your weakest thinking skills in the interests, strengths, and skills section. You might also find that those characteristics and traits that you see as most important about yourself probably do not rely on thinking skills in your areas of weakness.

This makes a lot of sense. For example, if one of your best characteristics is your friendliness or empathy for others, you have strengths in the thinking skill of self-awareness. If one of your best characteristics is open-mindedness, then you are also likely to have the thinking-skill strength of being flexible.

It is important to know that you have probably practiced some of those thinking skills more in the areas that you like than in those that you don't like. That's normal and to be expected. Throughout the rest of this book we'll show you how to pay attention to the ways that you use those thinking skills effectively while you are engaging in activities that "light up your brain." In addition, we'll discuss ways to practice these skills in areas that you don't necessarily like. If you could learn how to apply the same organizational skills you'd use to set up your Facebook page while writing a book report, you will probably be able to improve in these areas, as well.

Chapter 3
Organization

Where is My Stuff?

Michael was very excited about entering the eleventh grade at his high school. He had gotten his driver's license over the summer, and his parents had helped him to buy a used car that he could drive back and forth to school. He spent part of the summer rewiring the car so that he could use his iPod through the car speakers. Also, he cleaned up the car so that it would be comfortable for his friends that he would be driving to and from school.

While Michael didn't love school, he usually found that he did very well on tests but sometimes had difficulty with his homework. It wasn't because he couldn't do the homework, it was usually because he forgot about it or couldn't find it. His parents had always joked that Michael's room looked like a tornado had gone through it, and even in elementary school Michael's teachers always talked about his messy desk. Unfortunately, some of that same disorganization and sloppiness was beginning to find its way into Michael's car and his locker at school. His car became a new place to lose his homework or his books or even to misplace his cell phone and his iPod.

One morning as Michael was getting ready to pick up his friends and drive to school, he could not find the keys to his car or even his backup set. Unfortunately, he didn't know where his cell phone was either, and did not remember his friends' cell phone numbers so that he could inform them that he was running late. He became really upset with himself for his lack of organization and vowed that he was going to do something to prevent this from happen again.

Eventually he found his keys and picked up his friends, but they were all late to school. That evening, Michael sat down with his parents and talked about what he could do to get more organized. He and his parents recognized that he would probably never be the neatest and most organized person in the world but that they needed a few simple strategies so that he wouldn't misplace some of his basic tools for home and school.

His parents decided that they would designate a drawer in the kitchen for Michael to always put his keys, wallet, and cell phone. They also suggested to Michael that he should empty the glove box in his car and put all of his things away every time he returned home. Michael's parents bought him a new backpack that had four different sections to help him keep his homework and schoolwork organized. They also decided on a designated spot in his car and in his bedroom where he would put his backpack away on a regular basis. Using these ideas helped Michael a whole lot. After this, he rarely misplaced his keys, cell phone, iPod, or backpack. While his room is still a mess and it sometimes takes him a long time to find his homework in his backpack, he feels much better about himself and far less stressed by his disorganization.

▲▼▲▼▲▼▲▼▲▼

Keeping organized is really pretty easy when you don't have to keep track of much. When you were younger, even if you were disorganized it really didn't matter too much if you couldn't find some of your favorite Legos or if you misplaced some action figures or dolls. As an older kid, however, there are some things that you just don't want to lose. For example, it is really awful when you lose your cell phone and can't get in contact with some of your friends. It's also embarrassing when you show up for lacrosse or soccer practice without some of your equipment because you weren't able to find it.

Being organized is crucial in school. You need to be able to keep track of what you need to do and the materials and books to do them with when you have six or seven classes a day and sometimes homework in every single one of them. Simply put, if you want to be successful in school, you will need to be organized more than you have ever been before.

In this chapter we describe what is meant by the thinking skill of organization. We will help you to improve organization and other thinking skills with three easy steps: **Know**, **Show**, and **Grow**. First, we help you to **know** when you use organization. After that, we **show** you how it might help you. Then, most importantly, we **grow** the thinking skill by helping you to practice and apply it in your daily activities. Keep in mind that getting better at organization or any of the executive functioning skills is not just a matter of learning and understanding it; it is really about practicing and applying these skills. The more you practice, the better you will become.

What is Organization?

Organization is a skill that helps you put objects or thoughts into orderly and logical groupings. It helps you to find what you need at school, at home, and for other activities. Becoming organized requires that you gather what you need to cook a meal, do a project, or get ready for practice.

There are two types of organization skills: organization of yourself and organization of your materials. Organizing yourself helps you to know what you need to set and complete short- and long-term goals. Organizing materials is mostly about having what you need on hand so you can complete a task when you set your mind to it.

Organization is an activity that you need to do over and over again. Even if you know how to be organized, it doesn't help you very much if you don't make the effort to know where things are, put them away in their right place, and reorganize on a regular basis. Just because you cleaned and organized your room once doesn't mean that it is going to stay like that forever. People who regularly work on organizing usually find that it is easier to do simply because most things are already in their place.

KNOW: *Where Do You Use Organization?*

Organization is used in situations where you need to get yourself together or get a group of materials or objects together. Knowing where things are, how to get to them, and how to put them together is vital to achieving a goal. When organizing yourself you often need to use the skill of planning. When organizing materials you need to put them into an order, sequence, or a designated place. Organization is very helpful when you find yourself asking questions such as "Where are my favorite jeans?" or "What do I need to finish my homework or chore?" or "How can I organize my thoughts to write a book report?" When you find yourself asking these types of questions you are going to need the thinking skill of organization.

Here is a list of common situations and activities that require organization:

- Writing a book report or paper
- Cleaning your room
- Finding your homework assignments so that you can complete them
- Keeping track of possessions such as a cell phone, keys, iPod
- Knowing where to find your user names and passwords in case you forget them

- Getting the information and materials needed to complete a science project

- Having the tools and equipment available to complete a building project such as putting together a model, some shelves, or an art project

*Now that you **know** a little more about where to use the thinking skill of organization, we will help you to see how using the skill helps you to get things done, become more efficient, and avoid frustration.*

SHOW: *How it Helps*

When you are effectively using organization skills you know where your things are, don't waste time looking for them, and can more readily get things done. Organization can help you put together your ideas into something that makes sense to others, whether you are telling your friends about a recent adventure or writing a book report for your English class.

Organization helps you to complete chores and homework without wasting time looking for things or forgetting about something important. Organization helps you to reach goals by keeping objects or ideas in order. Organization can help you to examine a complicated situation and get the things you need to start on or complete a task. Being organized helps you to complete a writing assignment for school, be prepared with everything that you want to take with you for a family vacation, and get your schoolwork done efficiently.

Think about how organization might have helped you in the past. Maybe if you had kept better track of your iPod, you would not have lost it and wouldn't have had to spend another $200 to get another one. If you simply put your dirty clothes right into the laundry basket, you'd always have your favorite clothes clean and ready to wear to school, instead of having to wear dirty clothes or clothes that you dislike. Think about how frustrating it is when you spend twenty minutes looking through your backpack for your homework assignment when you could have already been finished with it if you had just put it into a homework folder and not had to look anywhere else.

Realistically, there are lots of reasons why people are not so organized. Many kids (and adults) are so busy and rushed, they simply don't take the time to put things away. Later when they go looking for those same things, they can't find what they want and waste countless hours looking for them. Other people are not really bothered if their room is messy or if the disorganization causes them a little extra stress. Sometimes people who are not that orderly or organized do not want to spend the time and energy necessary to be super organized. They believe that organized people actually put too much energy into being organized and see them as being compulsive in their need to know where things are. This is simply not for them.

If this describes you, then do not try to become a different person but simply develop a few basic organizational approaches that will make your life easier and reduce your stress and frustration when you can't find what you need. It is really not that hard, but it does require a commitment and action on your part. Organization doesn't just happen! You will need to organize and reorganize regularly, but you can limit the number of things that you want to spend your time organizing. The bottom line: you can't just say that you want to be more organized; you've got to do it.

GROW: *Using Organization in Daily Activities*

We want to give you some ideas about how to **grow** the thinking skill of organization. Some of you might want to try this on your own (Help Yourself). Others may need assistance from parents, teachers, or friends (Ask for Help). Still others might enjoy using ideas, techniques, and resources that can help develop organization skills (Helping Tools).

Organization is one of the executive functions that is easiest to improve. You can go to a store, buy some folders, desk or closet organizers, a new backpack, and you've already started. But you'll need to develop a system so that you can get organized and, most importantly, have an on-going method for staying organized. We want to stress that you do not need to devote your life to being organized and that you can improve your life with organization with a few simple strategies and consistent effort.

Before you start practicing organization skills, decide specifically what you would like to improve. The following list will help you to set clear and reachable goals. Check no more than two or three goals to work on at a time. If you want to get more organized, it is best to start with the basics. Once you are successful with these, proceed from there.

I want to improve my ability to:

_____ Find my homework

_____ Organize my written work

_____ Keep track of my equipment for sports teams and after school activities

_____ Know where my cell phone, iPod, and house keys are

_____ Keep track of and not lose my money

_____ Have a clean and more organized locker

_____ Have an organized bedroom where I can find things

_____ Know where my clothes are and put dirty clothes into a laundry basket

_____ Find my completed homework so that I can turn it in on time

_____ Have all materials for projects in one place before starting them

Help Yourself

1. Do it and re-do it. Organization is an action, it doesn't just happen. Once you have decided to organize something, it is important to update and reorganize it. It is probably best to start with something simple that you can take care of on a regular basis. For example, we might suggest that you try to organize your school backpack every Sunday night. This way you can throw away what you no longer need from the previous week and have a fresh start every Monday when the school week starts.

2. Create one special place where you keep your most important stuff (no more than three or four items) at home. Every time you return home from school, activities, or a friend's house, put your stuff in that spot. Usually it is best to have a place that is right near the entrance door to your house. Ask your parents if you can have a special drawer or shelf where you can put your cell phone, keys, wallet, iPod, and any other important personal items that you don't want to lose. You might also think about a regular place that you keep these things in you when you leave the house. For example, you might want to clip your cell phone onto a belt or use a particular pants pocket, backpack, or a purse to keep other items. Try to keep these things in their place when you are not at home so that you do not lose track of them.

3. Take some time to stop, think, and organize. Think about ways that organizing yourself or your stuff might make your life better. Don't organize for others, organize for yourself. If you get more stressed out over not being able to find your favorite jeans than your homework, then find a way to organize your clothes. While we are not trying to encourage you not to care about finding your homework, you will usually find that once you learn to organize yourself in one area, it becomes easier to do in another, more challenging area.

4. Learn how to organize your thoughts for written assignments at school. One of the most common difficulties for kids who have organizational problems is getting their thoughts together in an organized fashion for writing assignments. This is not easy, and there are actually complete books written about this subject; however, we have a couple of helpful hints for using technologies that you already have to improve writing skills. One strategy is to make sure that you have some type of voice recognition program or recorder on your cell phone or iPod. There are plenty of these available, such as Dragon Dictate for your iPod, and most cell phones have a tape recorder.

   When you are thinking about a paper or a project that you need to do, simply brainstorm your ideas onto your cell phone or iPod and later put them into a word processing document. You can always organize these ideas and add more ideas later. When you sit down to organize these ideas simply do some cutting, pasting and moving them around so that there is an orderly sequence to them. For instance, you might want to try using some type of electronic graphic organizer to help you organize your thoughts and get started on each of the paragraphs or sections of a report that you need to write. An awesome graphic organizer that is used in many schools throughout the country (maybe even yours) is a software package called Inspiration 9. Consider downloading a free trial to see if it helps and then ask your parents to consider purchasing a copy for your home computer. There are also some free graphic organizers available online, such as MindMapper, Eduplace, and Creatly.com.

Ask for Help

1. Kids who are disorganized usually have heard all about it from their parents, friends, or teachers. Interestingly, many kids who are disorganized see disorganization in their mom or dad. Just like you, your parents probably wish they were more organized and will be happy to help you buy organizational tools such as desk organizers, laundry baskets, or folders that might help you to organize your stuff. You might also have a very well-organized parent who could help you to come up with a few basic strategies for getting and staying organized.

2. Observe and rely upon your friends. Ask a friend who is very well organized for help. If you are lucky enough to have an organized friend in a bunch of your classes, see if you can get that friend to remind you of what you need to take home from school.

In today's world there is really no excuse for not knowing what your homework is. All you need to do is text your friends in your class and ask them what it is. Make sure you have a phone number for at least one person in each of your classes so you can always find out about your assignments.

Helping Tools

1. At its basic level, organization means that things have a place. One way to make yourself more organized is to have designated places for things that you own and for objects that are important to you. You might want to see if you can get a set a drawers or shelves for your room to keep your schoolwork and other materials organized. If you have a hard time finding clean clothes in your room, you might want to ask your parents to get you three laundry baskets, one for clean clothes, a second where you throw your dirty clothes, and a third where you put clothes that have been worn but that you might want to wear again before you get them washed. This simple system, while not always keeping your clothes unwrinkled, works for a lot of disorganized kids.

2. Use images and photographs to help you stay organized. If you cannot remember what drawers you put your t-shirt and socks into, take a digital picture of your socks and post it on your sock drawer. Digital pictures can also help you to remember the materials that you might need to complete a school project or what you will need to bring with you to practice everyday. Your cell phone is a great resource for taking pictures that

you can access regularly as reminders for tasks. For example, you can take a picture of your sports bag that includes your soccer cleats, socks, uniform, shin guards, and soccer ball. Develop a routine of looking at this image on your cell phone before you leave the house to make sure you have everything with you.

Chapter 4
Planning

What Should I Do?

Sarah recently decided that she wanted to become president of her eighth grade class. She thought that she had a very good chance of being elected because she was active in student council in the seventh grade and had a lot of great ideas about what would make her school better.

Part of Sarah's reason for running for president was that she had made a lot of new friends and felt as if she had become one of the more popular kids in her school. Being popular had its good and bad points. It made it so that Sarah had a lot of friends who wanted her to do things with them. However, combined with running for class president, playing on the school soccer team, and having a lot of homework, this caused Sarah to feel overwhelmed and stressed. Sarah didn't know what to do with her popularity. It was almost as if she had too many friends and not enough time for them. She didn't want to give up her interest in music, either. She had been playing the piano since she was 6 years old and really enjoyed practicing.

Sarah needed a plan. She needed to figure out how she could keep doing all of these activities and still enjoy them. She had to ask herself, "How am I going to do all of this stuff?" This helped her to start thinking about some of the steps that she could take to keep her life interesting and fun, but a little less overwhelming. The first thing she did was think of ways that she could get some of her homework done when she was otherwise just hanging around. She now does her math homework on the bus ride home from school. She also found that one great way to combine friends and school was to study for tests with some of her friends. Sarah asked her parents for assistance, as well, and they helped her to develop a great plan for running for class president.

Sarah also started to use her iPod for keeping track of her assignments and activities. She set up some alarms to remind her when she had projects due and when to practice the piano.

While Sarah is still really busy, she feels good about all of the great things that she is doing this year. And, by the way, she was elected president of her class, which has made her even more popular than ever.

▲▽▲▽▲▽▲▽▲▽

Remember when you were younger, say about 8 or 9? You didn't need to do much in the way of planning back then. If you are like most kids, your parents, teachers, or maybe an older sibling planned everything for you. They would tell you when you had soccer practice or when you were going to visit your grandparents. They probably woke you up in the morning and reminded you to do your homework before you went out to play after school. At school, your teacher assigned you homework that was uncomplicated and pretty easy, and you didn't have to plan how to do it. You simply completed the examples that she gave you or read a required book.

You probably also did not have as many things to do. Maybe you had just one after-school activity, such as taking guitar lessons. It was probably harder to get together with your friends, unless they lived in the neighborhood and you could just go outside and play with them. If you did something after school, you weren't the one who had to make arrangements for a ride or make plans for working on a school project or activity.

In your teen years, the need for planning becomes much greater than it was in the past. You need to balance more activities than ever before and probably have more responsibilities or chores at home. At school, your assignments aren't quite as easy or straightforward, either. You're given more projects that force you to figure out what it is you want to work on and what materials and approaches you'll need to go about doing it. If you want to be able to do well with the requirements of school, have time to hang out with your friends, and keep up with your activities, you need the thinking skill of planning.

What is Planning?

Planning helps you to figure out the steps you need in order to accomplish a goal, such as getting a job or saving enough money for a present for a friend. Planning requires that you think about what it is you want to do, consider the ways to get there, and take into account the obstacles that might get in your way.

Planning really involves thinking about the future. You need to have an idea about what you want to achieve and, more importantly, what you will need to do to make it happen. For example, if you want to try out for the soccer team in the fall, you probably want to get in shape by running and practicing drills throughout the summer so that you are ready when tryouts begin. Planning often involves prioritizing, or deciding what is the most important thing you want to do. It can also involve sequencing, or thinking about the order in which you should act.

Good planning requires that you think about all sides of a situation. You may need to make a good guess about possible outcomes and you should consider what to do if your plan does not succeed. For example, you might have a great idea about going out to the movies and ice cream with your friends but cannot get anyone's parents to drive you there. Unfortunately, there are many times when you might come up with a great plan but it doesn't get you where you want to go.

That's right! As important as planning is, it doesn't always result in achieving your goals. Many complications can arise that might be beyond your control. A plan to spend a day at the beach might be ruined by rainy weather. The sleepover that you were so excited about might be delayed because some of your friends got the flu. In fact, an important part of planning is being able to adjust your plans due to events that might be outside of your control.

Good planning can include using your own previous experiences or those of others to help you in the process. Using something you learned in the past to help you plan for current situations is often one of your best tools. Planning sometimes take patience, as well. Sometimes it means delaying the start of an activity so that you can have everything ready that is necessary to reach your goal.

KNOW: *Where Do You Use Planning?*

Planning is used in situations where you need to prepare for something. You often use planning when setting a goal for yourself or when someone else gives you a task or homework assignment that you need to complete.

Planning is helpful when you find yourself asking certain types of questions, for example, "How am I going to do that?" or "How can I get an 'A' in that class?" or "How am I going to get all of my homework done and still have time to go to the movies with my friends?" When you find yourself asking these types of questions, you are going to need the thinking skill of planning.

Here is a list of common situations and activities that require planning:

- Doing homework

- Preparing for and competing in a sporting event

- Organizing and cleaning your room

- Getting dressed

- Leaving enough time to complete tasks

- Completing tasks that require multiple steps

- Setting priorities

- Completing a lengthy project (e.g., putting together a model, creating an art project)

- Saving money to buy an expensive item (e.g., a videogame, an iPod, or a car)

- Doing a science project

- Studying for a test

- Writing a book report/paper

Now that you **know** a little more about where you use the skill of planning, we will help you to see how using this skill helps you to get things done, feel better about yourself, and just be happier. The next section **shows** how planning can help you.

SHOW: *How It Helps*

When planning works, it helps you to become more efficient and get things done. You will probably have more time to do fun things such as Facebooking your friends, shooting hoops, or just hanging out. Planning will definitely help you with projects for school such as a long book report or a science project. It will help you to leave enough time to complete the project and, more importantly, to plan the best sequence of steps for completing it.

Take a minute to think about how planning could help you in whatever you are doing today. Could better planning give you more time to have fun? Could it help you in your schoolwork? As we said earlier, you really need to think in order to plan. If you can get into the habit of stopping, thinking, and planning what you want to do, you are likely to find that accomplishing many of your goals will go more smoothly for you.

This is not to say that you should plan everything in your life. It is healthy to be spontaneous at times and to live "in the moment." In fact, sometimes the best plan is just to let things happen. Once you've learned the skill of planning, you will be better able to find a balance between "just doing it" and thinking about something beforehand.

The best way to get better at planning is to practice. The more planning becomes a habit for you, the more likely you will be able to use this skill when it is helpful and to ignore it when it is not.

GROW: *Using Planning in Daily Activities*

As we've told you throughout this book, if you believe that you can get better at something by working at it and practicing it, then you will **grow** the skill and get better at it. It's as simple as that. Certainly this is true of planning, because it helps you get used to thinking about what you want to do before jumping into it. When you first begin the planning process, consider a range of possible plans and then carefully make a decision to follow one specific plan. By doing this, you are going to have more success at reaching your goals. This does not mean that every plan you make will be a good one, nor does it mean that by simply planning you will reach your goals, but if you plan, you will have more success in reaching your goals over time

Before you start practicing planning skills, decide specifically what you would like to improve. The following list will help you to set clear and reachable goals. Check no more than three goals to work on at a time. It is difficult to work on too many at once, and part of your "planning" is to select the goals that are most important to you at this particular time.

I want to improve my ability to:

_____ Set long-term goals for myself

_____ Save money for something I really want

_____ Understand the steps I need to do my homework quickly and correctly

_____ Keep better track of my work

_____ Create a plan before writing an essay or working on a project

_____ Keep track of my responsibilities outside of school

_____ Get better at strategies while playing videogames

_____ Think about my future

_____ Know what books and materials I need for school projects

_____ Keep better track of my after-school schedule

_____ Think before I act

_____ Make plans to get together with my friends

_____ Think about the future, as well as the present

_____ Learn to put tasks in an order that helps me keep track and complete them

Help Yourself

1. Save for something big that you would like to buy. This is a great way to practice the skill of planning, as you need to figure out how much money you need to save, how you are going to get the money, and how you can avoid spending the money you have on other things. You might want to create a chart or log to help keep track of the money that you have saved. Some parents, after seeing their kid's demonstrated thoughtfulness and planning, may contribute to the total.

2. Practice your planning skills by helping someone else. Sometimes it is hard to look at all the things you need to do and to figure out how to do them. It may be easier to help someone like a younger sibling or a friend with planning tasks. While you are helping others, pay attention to the questions you ask them, what you need to learn about them and their activities, and, most importantly, how you need to help them in prioritizing and sequencing what they are doing.

3. Think big. Do some investigation into how a major production such as one of your favorite movies or videogames was produced. Realizing the many people, activities, and coordination efforts that went into creating this final product will give you a deeper appreciation for planning.

4. Think even bigger. Take an issue such as global warming, poverty, or world hunger and start thinking about the plans you would need to address these problems. While you are probably not going to come up with a plan that solves these problems, thinking about these worldwide difficulties will give you an opportunity to figure out what is most important and to practice setting a few goals and determining some initial steps you might take to achieve those goals.

Ask for Help

1. Ask for help. This is easy to do, but hard to follow, especially if you are asking your parents for help. However, sometimes just hearing a different perspective can be very useful. Rather than asking your parents to "tell you what to do," ask them if they can help you to plan for accomplishing a particular goal that you have in mind.

2. Watch how other people plan. Identify people in your life who are good at setting and accomplishing goals and watch how they do it. Ask them how they set goals and then look at their approach to achieving those goals. See if you can use some of their strategies and techniques in setting some goals of your own.

Helping Tools

1. Use technologies to help you in planning and remembering to do things. Most kids who are lucky enough to have a cell phone or an iPod know how powerful these gadgets are for planning. You can use them to schedule appointments, set alarms, or send yourself texts to serve as reminders about homework assignments and projects that you need to complete. You might also be able to get in touch with a Facebook friend to discuss assignments.

2. Create a master calendar of all of the events and activities that you have. Use this to write down deadlines for long-term assignments for school, a schedule for your sports teams, or to keep track of music lessons. Put the calendar in a place where you will see it every day. Some kids find that it is also helpful to have their parents keep the same type of calendar in a public place so that their parents can remind them about what they need to do. It can be useful to have a routine of "syncing" these calendars on a weekly basis.

Chapter 5
Focus

When You Have to Pay Attention

Rebecca was the best soccer player on her middle school team. She was entering the eighth grade, had played on travel soccer teams for many years, and was often recognized as the best player in her age group. She was hoping that her eighth grade coach would name her captain of the eighth grade team and was very disappointed when he named two of her teammates who were not nearly at the same playing level that she was.

Rebecca decided to ask the coach why she wasn't chosen. The coach, who really liked Rebecca a great deal, told her that he wanted the captains to be players who were always able to follow his instructions and to lead the team in drills during practice. Rebecca frequently did not seem to know what to do and appeared to be distracted when he was coaching the team. Rather than getting angry with the coach, Rebecca told him that she agreed with him and that it had always been difficult for her to remain focused on what she was doing.

She told the coach how, even in elementary school, her teachers would tell her parents that Rebecca was a nice kid but that she was always talking in class and often didn't pay attention to directions. She remembered that her elementary school teachers always needed to get her started on her assignments and then remind her to keep working so that she could complete them. She told the coach that she was a daydreamer and that sometimes when she was trying to listen to him, she found herself thinking about something that had happened during the day. She even told the coach that her friends had started to get upset with her for being distracted during conversations with her and that she often did not appear to be listening to them.

After the conversation with the coach, Rebecca decided that she wanted to do something about her focusing skills. She realized that she was extremely focused in some things, for example when she was actually playing soccer. This was part of what made her into such a great player. The fact that she could focus in some situations helped her realize that she needed to try to do more things that captured her interests and kept her attention.

She also needed to find ways to make herself be more focused in less interesting activities. She began standing in the front of the lines for soccer drills, where she would make herself stare at the coach or volunteer to be a leader in the drill so that she knew exactly what she needed to do. She also recognized that she needed some help getting started on schoolwork and other tasks, so she began asking her parents and teachers for suggestions on where and how she could get started in order to complete tasks more effectively. Just by being aware of her struggles with staying focused, Rebecca began to make some improvements. While she believed that being a bit of a daydreamer was always a part of who she was, she made enough improvement so that by mid-season her coach had made her a co-captain of the soccer team. In addition, her teachers all noticed her improvements and made comments about it on her report card.

▲▼▲▼▲▼▲▼▲▼

If you are a smart kid, and you probably are if you're reading this book, you didn't have to focus too much when you were in elementary school; in fact you might have been able to pay attention fifty percent of the time but knew ninety percent of the material. It is very different when you get to middle and high school. They usually teach you things that you didn't already know, and your teachers go so fast that if you are not paying attention the first time, you just might not get it at all. Suddenly, focusing fifty percent of the time no longer works for you. Not only are you missing out on learning new material, but you might also not be paying attention when your teacher gives you homework or important directions about a long-term project.

Your friends might begin to notice it as well, especially if you are always daydreaming or getting off topic in a conversation. As a teenager you are more likely to have serious and in-depth conversations with your friends, and they might not like it if it seems that you are not listening to them or don't care about what they are saying.

So as you can see, there are a lot of reasons that you want to improve your thinking skill of focus. We will help you to understand more about what focus is and what you can do to improve it in next few pages.

What is Focus?

Focus is the thinking skill that helps you get started on a task and keep your attention and effort to complete it. It helps you to stay on task even when there are many distractions.

Focus is about being in the present. Rather than thinking about the past or the future or letting your mind wander to something other than what you are doing, focus is about directing your attention. It helps you to get started more efficiently on what you want to do and helps you to sustain your effort and attention so that you can complete a task to the best of your ability.

Many teenagers have heard about people who have problems with their focus and are diagnosed with ADHD (Attention Deficit/Hyperactivity Disorder). Some people think that you can't focus on anything if you have ADHD and that no matter what you do you will always be distracted. This is not the case. Many people with ADHD or even milder attention problems have more trouble switching their attention from one activity to another or forcing themselves to tend to something that they experience as boring. Many people with attention and focusing problems report that their attention span is longer if something is of interest to them (this depends upon the person), such as video games, listening to music, reading, artwork, playing a sport, or building something. These people often report that they can become highly focused and have no difficulty in getting started and finishing what they intended to do in these activities.

KNOW: *Where Do You Use Focus?*

Focus is used in situations where you need to be able to start directly on a task and sustain your attention in the presence of distractions and where reaching a goal is important. It involves knowing what you need to get started on a task, deciding what to attend to, having the ability to return to an activity when you are interrupted, and putting forth the ongoing effort to stick with long-term goals.

Focus is helpful when you find yourself asking certain types of questions such as "What do I need so that I can get started on this work?"; "Which of the following things is most important for me to pay attention to right now?; and "How will I get back on track if I get interrupted?".

Here is a list of common situations and activities that require focus:

- Starting and completing chores that are boring or unpleasant
- Ignoring distractions when working on homework or cleaning your room
- Returning to do your homework when your little brother or sister bothers you
- Keeping your attention to instructions given by your teacher or coach
- Starting on your chores within a reasonable amount of time
- Being able to shift your attention from one thing to another when told to by a teacher or parent
- Being able to sit through meals, religious services, graduations, and weddings from start to finish
- Listening to someone else speak and then waiting to ask appropriate questions
- Ignoring other kids who are making noise in your class while continuing to pay attention to the teacher

SHOW: *How It Helps*

Focus helps you to learn. Simply put, if you are not paying attention, you are less likely to learn, whether at school, playing a videogame, or playing an instrument. Focus also helps you to tune into what is actually important. Often there are many things going on around you, such as noises outside or people talking, and focusing skills help you to prioritize which sounds and activities are most important to you in that given moment. Staying focused also helps you with your interactions with others. Kids who are able to focus on conversations with their friends are seen as good listeners and caring friends. For example, you become an important contributor when you are able to focus on a group project at school. On the flipside, if you are the type of friend who is always butting in on conversation before your friends have a chance to finish what they are saying, you may end up making your friends angry or make them feel unimportant.

If you have noticed that you have had a problem with focus for a long time, it is important for you to pay attention not only to the times that it is hard for you to focus, but also to the activities where it is easy for you to focus. These are the areas that you are going to want to pursue as you get older. For example, if you find that you focus very well when you are doing things with your hands, you might want to think about careers as a building contractor, an architect, or an artist. If you find that you are most focused when you are outdoors, you might want to think about being an oceanographer, a geologist, or a gym teacher. If you find that you focus best when you are playing video or computer games you may want to think about a technology-based job or working with film and other media. While it is still important to focus in the classroom and in the things that don't interest you as much, as you get older it becomes even more important for you to find the areas where focus is not a problem for you.

GROW: *Using Focus in Daily Activities*

Getting better at focusing skills requires a combination of knowledge, self-examination, and effort. While you probably know some kids who also take medication to improve their focus due to having an Attention Deficit/Hyperactivity Disorder, there are many other ways that you can change your behavior and your approach to learning to improve your focusing skills. Improving your focusing skills doesn't mean that you are always going to be able pay attention or that you won't get bored or distracted when you are doing something that you don't like. However with some effort, you will definitely be able to improve your focusing skills and, most importantly, start and complete things so that you are happy with your results.

Before you start practicing your focusing skills, it is best to decide the areas where that you would like to improve. The following list will help you to set clear and reachable goals. Check no more than two or three goals to work on at a time. It is difficult to work on too many at once, and you will need to "focus" on what is most important, just like you will need to in any situation involving your focusing skills.

I want to improve my ability to:

_____ Continue working on tasks that I find dull or boring, such as homework

_____ Stay on task while working in groups

_____ Listen to my teachers more carefully in following directions

_____ Complete lengthy projects by starting them on time and sustaining my effort

_____ Keep trying to work on something when it is very boring

_____ Keep practicing and stick to things that are difficult to master such as learning an instrument or playing a sport

_____ Learn how to get started promptly rather than delaying

_____ Learn how to stop one activity when it's time to start another

_____ Stop daydreaming in class

_____ Keeping up the energy and effort needed to finish a goal

Help Yourself

1. Break tasks into smaller pieces that can be completed in one sitting. For example, work on jigsaw puzzles that are suitable for your age and that increase in difficulty. If you are 12 years old you might start with a puzzle that has two hundred pieces and, as you get older, move up to larger puzzles that might include five hundred pieces. Try to sit for sustained periods to work on the puzzle. It might also be useful to work on the puzzle

with a sibling or to break up the puzzle into components so that each of you is working on a different part. Think about how breaking up a large task such as a puzzle may be similar to working on the steps towards completing a long-term project at school.

2. Participate in activities that require your full attention. For example, if you are going to play baseball or softball, play catcher, pitcher, or first base where you have to pay attention non-stop more during the game, as opposed to outfield positions, where you might have time to daydream. In music, play instruments that are a regular part of the orchestra, rather than instruments that are simple, but rarely used. If you choose to act in a play, try for a lead role, where you realize that everyone will be watching what you do.

3. Find interesting and stimulating activities to do after a boring or mundane task. For example, you may dread doing your math homework, so learn to reward yourself by playing a videogame, going outside to shoot baskets, or texting your friends after you have completed it.

4. Control your distractions. Lots of kids who have attention problems make it worse for themselves by having things like their cell phones or Facebook page open while they are trying to concentrate on something else. Restrict yourself from things that might distract you and specify the amount of time, say twenty or thirty minutes, that you can choose to focus on completing your homework. As you get better at this, increase the amount of time that you will keep distractions away from yourself while you are focusing on your homework or other less preferred tasks.

Ask for Help

1. In school, it may be useful for you to sit toward the front of the class. It is harder to become distracted or to tune out a teacher who is looking at you during the whole class period. While this may not be fun for you, it is a valuable technique that works for many people in maintaining their attention. Also, by being in front of the class you may be more likely to engage in classroom participation. Just talking and interacting tends to help people keep their focus in the classroom.

2. Ask your parents or teachers to give you gentle reminders to tune in and pay attention to what you are doing. Once you recognize that you have a problem with focus and explain this to the adults in your world, they are more likely to be understanding and, in turn, to encourage you. If you inform your teachers that you get distracted and wish that you didn't, they will be more likely to give you a gentle reminder to get back to work or even give you some ideas about how to get started on or to complete a more difficult assignment in the classroom.

You might also wish to ask your parents and teachers for advice for getting started on projects. Kids with focusing difficulties often struggle to complete tasks because they get caught up in not knowing where to start. Getting a little outside help or hints about a way that you could start your project can work wonders for you.

Helping Tools

1. Technologies are great for helping kids to focus. Cell phones and iPods are particularly good for setting alarms and timers that can alert you to get started on something or pace your time according to how long you want to work on a set task. Many kids who have difficulties with focus also find that listening to some music (not watching the television) can be helpful for them in sustaining their focus. Most of the time we find that music without words is best for helping people to focus. It tends to block out other sounds but doesn't require a great deal of focus in and of itself. While most teenagers don't like classical music or jazz, you might find that this is the type of music that actually works best for helping your focus.

2. Search for technologies that help you to sustain your attention for learning. For example, many kids who have problems in sustaining their attention while reading a long book find that they do very well listening to an audio book instead. You might also find apps that practice language skills in a way that is more interesting and engaging than your typical studying. Watching DVDs that cover subjects such as biology, astronomy, geology, history, and social studies is a great tool for developing broader knowledge about a subject and encouraging your interests in the books and materials that you are covering in school.

Chapter 6
Time Management

When You've Got Too Much to Do

Ashley is always late. She is late for school, late for soccer practice, and late meeting her friends. Up until recently no one would get too upset with her because Ashley was friendly and always got along with everyone. Unfortunately, her high school vice-principal is not nearly as understanding as her teachers and school administrators have been in the past. After she was late for school for the tenth time this year, the vice principal called Ashley into his office and informed her that she would be serving detentions for every subsequent tardy. As a result, she served ten after school detentions over the next month. Ashley's parents were upset with her for getting so many detentions and, maybe more importantly, Ashley was upset with herself. She missed many opportunities to get together with friends and was late to soccer practice six times due to her detentions.

Ashley began to think about what she could do to manage her time more effectively. It wasn't that she was purposely late or that she didn't care; instead, it was because she didn't pay very much attention to time and became easily distracted when she was getting ready to do something. In the morning it was not at all unusual for Ashley to start texting her friends or take an extra long shower. Problems with being late and managing her time were also making it so that she wasn't finishing her homework until very late at night, which resulted in her going to bed later and being tired in the morning when she had to wake up.

Ashley decided to do something about her chronic lateness and difficulties in managing her time. In order to reduce her tendency to be late in the morning she began to prepare everything she needed for school the night before, so that in the worst case scenario, she could simply wake up in the morning, put on some clothes, and grab her backpack and lunch to get to school on time.

She also examined the types of things that were distracting her from getting things done in a timely fashion and decided that she would try to eliminate some of these distractions when she needed more time. She made decisions like putting her cell phone into her backpack so that she wouldn't have access to it in the morning or when she was doing homework.

She also began to set some goals for herself in an effort to force herself into completing tasks more quickly. For example, she routinely began to do her homework half an hour before her family served dinner so that she had a limited amount of time to sustain her effort and focus. She also began to think about how long something might take before beginning it. In the past, Ashley would just jump into something and not be realistic about the amount of time it would take her to complete a task on time.

Ashley began doing much better about being on time as a result of these decisions. She is still occasionally late, and sometimes her friends are a little bit frustrated when they are left waiting to meet her. However, she has not had any further detentions and she actually finds that she has much more time to do the things she wants to do now that she manages the time she has.

▲▼▲▼▲▼▲▼▲▼

Managing your time was probably a lot easier for you when you were younger because you didn't have as many things to do. A lot of times it didn't matter how long it took you to do something, and most of the things that you had to do only required a little bit of your time. You probably also had a lot more direction and supervision from your parents and teachers. They would set time limits for you and maybe even sit down to help you get your homework done or get you started on a project for school.

As you get older time management becomes a very important part of getting things done that you have to do, while also having time left over for the things that you want to do. If it takes you four hours to do your homework every night, then you are not going to have much time to go on Facebook, practice your guitar, or go out with your friends. As you get into your teen years, some of the requirements of school can become particularly problematic for time management, which makes it even more important to manage your time effectively.

If you want to improve your time management you must first improve your awareness of time and develop a sense of urgency. This sense of urgency helps you to be able to prioritize what is important, choose what to do, and be efficient in your efforts to complete a task in a timely manner

What is Time Management?

Time management is an executive functioning skill that helps you to be efficient in how you start and complete tasks. It involves the ability to respond to things in a timely fashion. Time management helps you estimate the amount of time necessary to complete tasks and gives you the ability to make and follow a schedule.

It requires monitoring and paying attention to the time and effort you put into things. You need to have a sense of the relative urgency of tasks; in other words you don't need to stress out about doing things, but you do need to be aware of time constraints and adjust your priorities accordingly.

To use time management skills effectively you will use other thinking skills such as the capacity to sustain your focus on a task as well as your organization and planning skills. Good time management skills also involve being able to prioritize. At some point you are going to find that you simply have too many things to do and that only a superman or superwoman could get them all done in time. On these occasions you will have to decide what you think is most important and recognize that other things will just have to wait.

Even if you have the best time management skills in the world, there will be times that life just gets in the way. For example, you might always be ready to get to school on time, but one day your parent's car doesn't work so you get there late. Or you set aside plenty of time to get your homework done at night but the Internet isn't working in your house and therefore sets you back. While you can't prepare for everything, if you are using good time management skills most of the time you will leave yourself plenty of time to complete tasks with time to spend on the things you really like to do.

KNOW: *Where Do You Use Time Management?*

Time management is used in situations where you have deadlines or a schedule and need to accomplish tasks in an efficient manner. Time management is a very important tool when you need to determine priorities and not waste time working on things that may be unnecessary.

Time management is a key skill for completing homework and chores. Also, if you have an afterschool or weekend job, it is a highly valued skill for both for yourself and your employer. For you, it helps you to make time for a paying job while still being able to hang out with your friends. For your boss, it will be profitable to have you "working smart" and efficiently.

Time management is also helpful when you find yourself asking questions such as "How long will this take me?" or "What is the fastest way to get my homework done so that I will have time to hang out with my friends?"

Here is a list of common situations and activities that require time management:

- Studying for a final exam

- Using a calendar

- Doing your chores

- Going to bed and waking up on time

- Determining how long an activity will take

- Determining how much time it will take to run an errand or complete your homework

Now that you **Know** a little more about where to use the skill of time management, we will help you to see how using the skill helps you to get things done and become more efficient. The next section **shows** how time management can help you.

SHOW: *How It Helps*

When your time management skills are effective, they help you to get things done efficiently, complete your homework without delay, and have lots of time to do the things that you truly enjoy. Once you have mastered the art of time management you will usually know how long something will take you so that you can make better plans for something else later in the day. Using time management in long-term projects will help you not to be stressed out at the end of the project because you will easily have gotten it done by the deadline.

When time management skills are not working, you may find that it might take you far too long to complete the things that you don't want to do. You will tend to exaggerate how long something will take you or underestimate the amount of time it will take, not leaving yourself enough time to complete it.

Time management can help teenagers who are involved in many activities. If you regularly play an instrument or are on a school sports team, you are probably very busy and may struggle to keep up with your schoolwork without using good time management skills. If you are someone who likes to spend a lot of time with your friends, play an occasional videogame, or want to have time to Facebook your friends, you probably need to use your time effectively.

It is important to understand that not every situation calls for time management skills. When you are spending time hanging out with your family, enjoying a good conversation with your friends, reading a great book, or listening to your favorite music you may not want to pay attention to time. Sometimes simply being in the moment is the best thing to do and can help you to manage stress and unwind.

GROW: *Using Time Management in Daily Activities*

Time management is about having a sense of urgency and awareness of time. You need to be able to estimate the amount of time a task will take you, have the capacity to have prioritize, and work at a speed that fits the situation. You also need to recognize where and when you need to apply these skills.

If you find yourself frequently late, rushing to complete your schoolwork, or stressed by having too much to do and too little time to do it, you can benefit from learning time management skills. Fortunately, there are a number of time management strategies, tools, and technologies that can to improve these skills

The following list will help you to set clear and reachable goals. Check no more than three goals to work on at a time. It is difficult to work on too many at once, and the capacity to prioritize is an important part of developing time management skills. Prioritizing will help you to select the goals that are most important at this time.

I want to improve my ability to:

_____ Make and follow a daily schedule

_____ Complete my homework on time

_____ Finish my chores more quickly

_____ Have more time to spend with my friends

_____ Make myself get started on chores and activities that I do not like to do but have to do

_____ Work better under pressure

_____ Be able to complete a long-term project before the last minute

_____ Get enough sleep at night so that I wake up refreshed

_____ Be better at estimating how long homework and other assignments will take

Help Yourself

1. Learn how to prioritize. First you need to stop, think, and figure out what is the most important thing to do when you have a number of competing tasks. This is not as easy as it sounds. Sometimes it helps to make a list where you can arrange and rearrange items in order of importance.

2. Teach yourself to estimate how long something will take you to do. Before starting a homework assignment, cleaning your room, or some other task, write down how long it will take you. When you are done, check how close you were to your estimate. If you write this down and keep track of it on a regular basis, you will get better and better at

estimating how long tasks will take to complete. This will help you to make sure that you have enough time to complete what you need to do so that you will have time for what you want to do.

3. Give yourself a reward for finishing something quickly and efficiently. For example, set a realistic amount of time to complete your homework and if you are able to do so, reward yourself with an activity you enjoy such as texting your friends, having a snack, or hanging out with friends.

4. Create a schedule for yourself. Post a 2x3 foot calendar in your bedroom that is highly visible to you. At the beginning of each month put down all of your regular commitments such as music lessons, religious classes, sports practices, and games. You may want to do some type of color-coding to recognize busy as opposed to stress-free days. You can also use this calendar for scheduling long-term school projects, family vacations and other important events.

5. Practice your time management skills by helping someone else prioritize. Sometimes it is easier to help a friend, sibling, or even a parent to prioritize what they need to do and manage their time. When helping another person with managing their time, it is necessary to ask questions to help them clarify what is most important for them to do and have them estimate the amount of time it will take them to complete each of the tasks.

Ask for Help

1. Ask your parents for help in developing a family schedule of events. Have a family schedule that lists priorities, appointments, and special activities will be helpful. Using a large, visible family calendar is a great visual tool.

2. In school, ask teachers for help when it comes to managing long term projects. Most teachers are very willing to help you think through the various steps that you will need to complete a long-term assignment. Some teachers will provide you with a schedule for getting materials, creating a rough draft, and getting feedback from the teacher. If not, ask your teacher for help in this way so that you have more than the start and end date available.

Helping Tools

1. Use your cell phone. Cell phones are a great invention for problems with time management. You can program your cell phone with alarms and messages that alert you when you need to complete something. You can use your cell phone as a timer to help keep track of how long a task is taking you or to remind you that you need to complete it in a certain amount of time. Smart phones have a number of other features and apps that can be used to help with time management.

2. Use an agenda. In all likelihood your parents and teachers have been trying to get you to use an agenda or calendar for scheduling your school assignments for many years. Believe it or not, this is really a great idea. As you get older, it is virtually impossible to remember everything that you need to do. Without remembering what you need to do, you have no chance of being able to prioritize or manage your time effectively.

The key to having an agenda is to make sure that you put everything in it and that you check it regularly, crossing out what you have already completed and re-prioritizing what needs to get done by writing new items as they arise. It's all about using and referring to your agenda. It is not enough just to put down what you need to do without looking at it again. You need to your agenda as a guide and a tool to improve your awareness of what you need to do and where you are in the process of doing it.

Chapter 7
Self-control

How to Stop, Relax, and Decide

Matthew is one of the most popular kids in his school. He is friendly, full of energy, funny, and very athletic. Most of his teachers really like him, although sometimes they need to ask him to get back to work in class and stop talking to his friends.

Matthew is also one of the best football players on his high school team. He is very competitive and uses his energy to encourage his teammates to do their best. Occasionally he can get too competitive, and he has problems controlling his emotions. He hates to lose, and while this helps him put forth his best effort, his behavior after his team has lost upsets his coaches and his parents.

Matthew has also recently been having problems with a few of his teachers at school. He has always been a class clown, but most of his former teachers liked him so much that they didn't mind when he would do something silly or blurt out things in the middle of class. However some of his new teachers are much more serious and do not want Matthew's behavior interfering with the class. As a result, he has had a few detentions, and at one point his football coach held him out of a game because of his poor sportsmanship after the team's loss.

Matthew recognized that these behaviors were not new. Sometimes he would act out in anger towards his parents when he did not get his way at home. There had also been other occasions when he tended to act before thinking at school and sporting events. Matthew recognized his difficulty with self-control and decided to do something about it.

First, Matthew worked on controlling his emotions. He thought long and hard about the types of situations that tended to set him off and decided that the best way to display better sportsmanship and control his feelings at football games was to put all of his energy into the game and then let it go afterwards. After talking with his best friend, he came to an understanding that there are many times in life when things didn't go the way he wanted and that if he were really going to be happy, he'd have to be better at dealing with disappointment.

Matthew took a different approach to controlling his behavior. He developed a few strategies to stop himself from acting before thinking in class. When he got the feeling that he was going to blurt something out, he learned to put his hand over his mouth until the urge went away. He also decided to learn how far he could go with his different teachers, so that he didn't find himself in more trouble.

Matthew's behavior change has become very evident to his coaches and teachers. His coaches decided to make him into a defensive captain, and his teachers, who had given him detentions, began to compliment him for his performance in school.

▲▽▲▽▲▽▲▽▲▽

As you get older, the need for better self-control goes hand-in-hand with accepting more responsibility in your life. One of the reasons that 10-year-olds are not allowed to drive is not simply because they are too small, but also because they may not have adequate self-control to make good decisions while driving. Teenagers who lack self-control are often described as being immature.

Self-control becomes an important part of making good choices regarding drugs and alcohol, being truthful to your parents, and avoiding high-risk behavior. Skills of self-control help you to be able to stop, think rationally about what you want to do, and make better decisions.

What is Self-control?

Self-control involves the ability to manage your feelings effectively. Individuals with good self-control tend to have a consistent mood. Self-control also helps you to sustain your effort in the face of frustration and difficulty.

A second component of self-control involves the ability to stop or delay an action and to think before acting. Self-control is an important skill for being safe, displaying appropriate behavior, and making good decisions that lead to better problem solving. Self-control helps you to size up and understand a situation before you do anything.

There are some situations in which it is very hard to exert self-control, and it may not be necessary to do so. For example, if your sports team wins a championship, you might want to jump for joy. If a girlfriend or boyfriend breaks up with you and you're feeling very sad, it may be important to let go of your feelings and allow yourself to cry or experience sadness. However in both of these situations, if you let it go too far or too long, your loss of self-control begins to hurt you.

Self-control involves a sense of maturity. For example, a 2-year-old displaying a temper tantrum is considered to be normal, but a 15-year-old acting the same way is immature. As you get older, self-control needs to be imposed from within. What that means is that you need to regulate your own actions and not rely on your parents and teachers, who made the rules for your behavior and monitored your actions so closely in your younger days.

KNOW: *Where Do You Use Self-control?*

Self-control is often used in situations involving other people. For example, you use self-control when you're able to stop yourself from talking and take turns in a conversation or game. You also use self-control when you're able to wait until someone finishes a question before you start to answer or when you raise your hand in class rather than blurt something out. Self-control is also involved in emotional situations. You are able to take a deep breath and control your actions and feelings when somebody says something hurtful to you, rather than becoming defensive, angry, or lashing out at that person. Self-control helps you with disappointment when your parents tell you "no" or when a friend cancels a long-awaited activity with you.

Self-control is helpful when you find yourself asking questions such as, "Why did my teacher pick on me for talking when everyone else was talking in class?" or "Why do my parents say 'no' when all my friends are allowed to do something?" When you find yourself asking these types of questions, you are going to need the thinking skill of self-control.

Here is a list of common situations and activities that require self-control:

- Waiting to raise your hand before speaking in class

- Stopping and looking over your answers on a test before handing it in

- Taking responsibility for your actions when you have done something wrong

- Taking turns when playing a game and letting others have their turn

- Putting on all of your safety equipment such as your helmet before you get on your bike

- Completely reading the directions before taking a test or starting a project

- Stopping yourself from having a temper tantrum when you do not get what you want

- Not hitting your younger brother when he has broken something of yours

- Not overreacting to a situation that does not go your way

SHOW: *How It Helps*

When you are able to use the skill of self-control your life tends to be more in balance. You tend not to have as many highs and lows where you can become very angry and frustrated when things do not go the way you would like. Also, if you're feeling upset or down, self-control skills help slow you down enough to develop a plan to change the situation.

Self-control will probably help you in your relationships with your friends, as well. If your emotions are always getting the best of you, you react and get easily hurt by the drama that occurs and probably experience a lot of tension with your friends. On the other hand, if you don't let the little stuff bother you, you tend to be happier and less likely to find that you get into fights and conflicts with your friends.

The first step for improving your self-control skills is your ability to see where a situation causes trouble for you. Once you do that, you'll be able to learn ways to improve your ability to problem-solve and deal with difficult situations. Self-control can then help you to employ other thinking skills such as planning, organization, and time management in a way that is more effective.

GROW: *Using Self-control in Daily Activities*

A part of improving your self-control skills is simply getting older and being more mature. As you move into your late teen years, you'll find that making good decisions and thinking before acting become easier for you. However, it still requires that you are thoughtful and actively work on improving your self-control skills. By definition, self-control involves a decision on your part to improve you.

The following list will help you to set clear and reachable goals. Check no more than three goals to work on at a time. It is difficult to work on too many at once, and part of practicing self-control skills is to consider the areas that are most crucial for your growth and development.

I want to improve my ability to:

_____ Be more responsible for my decisions

_____ Be more relaxed and less reactive to criticism

_____ Be able to control my emotions in competitive situations

_____ Be more optimistic and stay positive about things, even after something bad happens

_____ Be able to wait my turn in conversation

_____ Display the ability to control my emotions when someone is arguing with or being critical of me

_____ Consider safety issues before engaging in risky behavior

Help Yourself

1. Learn to talk to yourself. Talking to yourself does not mean that you walk around your friends and family speaking out loud and making a fool of yourself; instead, it means learning how to use self-talk to direct yourself and make better decisions. You may wish to use it in situations that might be emotional or confrontational. You can learn to make statements such as, "Calm down," or "Take it easy." You may also use self-talk to restrain yourself by engaging in activities such as counting to 10 before you say something or telling yourself, "Listen," so you don't talk until someone has finished a conversation with you.

2. Learn to restrain yourself physically. We don't mean to wrap yourself up so that you look silly, but to use subtle tools that can help you restrict your activity or your talking. One simple technique is to put your hand over your mouth when you want to make sure you don't blurt out an answer or interrupt someone. Another technique to restrain your physical activity is to sit on your hands while you are on a chair, put your hands in your pocket when you're standing up, or fold your hands together to stop yourself from acting out in other settings.

3. Learn breathing and relaxation techniques. These techniques actually work if you know how to use them. While they are not guaranteed to make you totally relaxed or to stop you from losing self-control later, they can often help you make better decisions. One simple breathing technique is to take a very deep and extended breath in through your mouth. This breath can last as long as ten seconds, until you fill your lungs and abdomen with air. Try to hold your breath for five seconds or more and then slowly breathe out through your mouth. If you find yourself pushing the air out too fast, you've held your breath too long. Do this three to four times as slowly as you can and then respond to the situation.

4. Learn to think happy thoughts. Find a few images or situations you can easily place in your mind's eye. Make it so that you can easily access them. For example, this could include visions of having fun at the beach, doing a favorite activity, or skiing or snowboarding down your favorite mountain.

Ask for Help

1. Think about the people you can talk to when you're feeling really upset. When you find yourself in that situation, actively seek them out. If they are not around you at the time, take a break and text them or call them on the phone. Get their input about how to react to a particular situation.

2. Identify friends, family members, or teachers for whom you have a great deal of respect in the way that they solve problems and deal with people. Observe how they handle difficult people and situations. If you find yourself struggling with issues of self-control, engage them in a conversation about what their strategies are and how they handle frustration and upsetting situations. Many people find that simply talking to others who display certain skills helps them to be able to model their approach when facing difficult situations.

Helping Tools

1. Put yourself in situations where you are likely to be frustrated and then learn how to deal with them. One simple and fun example is to play video games that can be frustrating and difficult to learn. Talk to your friends or find a popular video game that is well-liked by others but is difficult to master. Play the game and recognize that you are likely to encounter all types of obstacles to success. Learn how to find ways to deal with the frustration (other than throwing the controller) and think about how this might help you in other aspects of your life.

2. Help your parents or other adults learn how to use their latest electronic gadget. When your parents get a new cell phone or DVR, assist them in setting it up and learning how to use it. In all likelihood, you won't know how to use all of the features and will make some mistakes in learning how to master this new technology. Try to recognize that you can learn from your mistakes and that part of the process of getting better at things is to make mistakes. Learning to change your approach from these mistakes is a lesson that can easily be applied to other situations in life.

Chapter 8
Flexibility

Try Something New

Jacob recently started seventh grade at his new middle school. He is finding it hard to adjust to new teachers, the new kids from other elementary schools, and the heavier workload at school. Jacob has always been an excellent student and has always liked his teachers, but he is becoming frustrated and angry with some of his new teachers, who he feels are critical of his work. His parents have noticed that he seems angry at home, as well, as he has been fighting with his younger sister and arguing more frequently with his parents.

Jacob keeps saying that he wishes things were like they were at his elementary school, where he had only a few teachers, always knew what was expected of him, and usually had his best friends in his classes. In middle school, he is finding that teacher expectations and grading strategies are different than what he is used to, but he hasn't figured out what he needs to do to meet those expectations. When he began getting Cs on some of his papers he became angry with some of his teachers and refused to talk to them about what he could do to improve his grades.

Jacob became "stuck" on the idea that he didn't like anything about his new school and found himself wishing he were back in the sixth grade. He began to refuse to do some of his homework and arguing with some of his teachers.

Jacob found it interesting that his best friend Christopher was truly enjoying middle school. Christopher told Jacob that he liked having a bunch of different teachers and going from class-to-class and enjoyed meeting new kids from the other schools and making new friends. He also talked to Jacob about the different after-school activities and encouraged Jacob to go with him and join the cross country team.

At first, Jacob didn't want to hear what Christopher was saying. Then he began to realize that he was not being very flexible in his thinking. Wanting things to be like they were in the sixth grade just wasn't going to happen. He thought about how he could adapt to the new situation and shift his thinking so that he could begin to enjoy some of the cool things in middle school.

Jacob then decided to join the cross country team and began meeting a lot of new kids that were in his classes. He decided that he would ask his teachers why he was getting Cs. He found out that each of his teachers had different expectations for him in the classroom and that once he began to understand that he needed to take different approaches with each of his teachers, his grades went up to As and Bs. He found that by adapting to new situations rather than being stuck and inflexible, he was much happier, made new friends, and got better grades.

▲▼▲▼▲▼▲▼▲▼

When you were younger, you probably didn't need to adapt and be flexible to new situations because there simply weren't that many of them. Not only did you have fewer choices about what to do, most young kids simply did what their parents or teachers told them to do. You also had fewer opportunities to do things. In school, you were in one class with one teacher. At home, you would stick around your house or neighborhood and not have nearly as many activities as you do now in middle school or high school.

Being flexible and adapting to new situations and challenges becomes a very important skill when you get older. Things tend to become more complicated in social relationships. There is often more drama and conflicts. You may have to be flexible with your scheduling, quickly shifting from one activity to another, and you are likely to find yourself in new situations in which you have no experience.

In order to get better at flexibility, you'll need to recognize where and how you use this skill but also have the willingness to change your approaches from the past and try new ways of dealing with your world. The more willing you are to be flexible, the better you will become at that skill.

What is Flexibility?

Flexibility helps you to adjust to unexpected events and to things that may disappoint you. It helps you to adapt to situations such as when your friend cancels a sleepover at your house or when the swimming pool is closed because of a rainstorm.

Being flexible doesn't only help you in solving problems and adapting to new situations, it's also an important tool for being happy. Sometimes kids and teenagers think that everything in their life will go the way that they want it to. Well, we have some sad news for you, "happily ever after" happens only in fairy tales. Hopefully most of your life will go the way you want it to, but it is important to be flexible when you experience sadness and disappointment. There is some good news in all of this. By understanding that sometimes things won't go so well, you can learn to adapt and make the best of a situation.

KNOW: *Where Do You Use Flexibility?*

Flexibility comes into play when you encounter new situations or problems that need to be solved. Most often, people try solutions that have worked for them in the past. But if these situations no longer work, you need to be flexible and try something new. You may need to change a routine that you were comfortable with or modify your way of looking at a problem. You know that you need to be more flexible when you repetitively make the same mistake or keep getting in trouble for the same thing.

Flexibility is also needed when it comes to dealing with friends. Getting along with others involves some give and take. As you get older and encounter a lot more kids in school and other activities, you need to learn how to deal with other kids that you may not really like.

Flexibility is also an important skill for being able to change what you are doing in any particular moment. For example, it is a very important skill to transition from having fun while playing a videogame to getting yourself ready to practice an instrument or have dinner with your family. Flexibility also helps you to transition from one activity to another at school, whether it's going from class to class or needing to adapt to the different expectations of six or more teachers in the middle school and high school setting.

Flexibility is helpful when you find yourself asking questions such as, "How can I do that differently?" or "What can I do now that my plans are ruined?" or "What else can I do, or who else can I call?"

Here is a list of common situations and activities that require self-control:

- Trying a new activity
- Adjusting to new teachers or substitutes
- Dealing with a change in plans

- Shifting from a concrete/rigid approach to something more flexible

- Being able to accept "no" as an answer

- Learning from making mistakes

- Dealing with transitioning from one activity to another

- Seeing someone else's point of view

- Changing your approach when you are told you are wrong

SHOW: *How It Helps*

When flexibility works, it helps you adapt to new situations, not get stuck with old routines, and more readily deal with frustration. By being flexible, you will be able to deal better with disappointment and change. You will learn how to find positive aspects of difficult situations and try new approaches.

Think about how flexibility might have helped you with your experiences in the past. Could improving your flexibility have helped you when you felt criticized by a parent or teacher? Could being more flexible have helped you to adjust more quickly to a situation so that instead of feeling anger and disappointment about a change in plans, you simply found something else to do?

Being flexible does not mean that you should walk around saying "whatever" However, there are times when your choices and actions may not be working and you need to adapt. The toughest part of using flexible problem solving skills is being able to know when to "stay the course" and when to change. Sometimes you have to stop and ask yourself if what you are doing is helping or hurting you. If it's not helping, it may be time for the thinking skill of flexibility.

The more you use the skill of flexibility, the better you will get at applying it in new situations. You will find that flexible thinking is a key component of solving problems. For those of you who play videogames, think about how you need to be flexible and try different approaches in order to beat a challenging game. If you get stuck using the same approach, you will never get past the first few levels. Similarly, when it comes to complex problems that you will encounter in school and in the real world, you will need to use more creativity, perspective-taking, and feedback in order to reach your goals.

GROW: *Using Self-control in Daily Activities*

Being flexible actually makes your life richer. This doesn't necessarily mean that you will have more money, but that people who are creative and adapt to new situations may have a broader and wider set of experiences in life. By being flexible you are more likely to try new foods and activities. You will be more willing to go to strange and exotic locations, meet people who are different from you, and take on new challenges knowing that you may or may not succeed.

Before you start practicing flexibility skills, decide specifically what you would like to improve. The following list will help you to set clear and reachable goals. Check no more than three goals to work on at a time. It is difficult to work on too many at once, and part of being flexible is recognizing that you may choose some goals now and then decide to change them later.

I want to improve my ability to:

_____ Learn from my mistakes

_____ Accept criticism

_____ Be creative

_____ Adapt to new situations

_____ Deal with changes in my routines

_____ Handle events that did not turn out the way I expected them to

_____ Deal with teachers or authority figures who are unfair

_____ Handle it when my parents say "no"

_____ Deal with disappointment from my friends

_____ Become better at problem solving

Help Yourself

1. Try things that you haven't done before just so that you can have new experiences. Try some new foods, new activities, or a new game to practice being more flexible.

2. Teach yourself to be physically relaxed. Interestingly, physical relaxation that you improve by doing yoga, stretching, or exercise can lead to a mindset of peacefulness. By being physically relaxed and calm, you are more likely to be flexible in your thinking.

3. Recognize that you change on a regular basis and that your problem-solving and thinking are already capable of change. This may not be evident to you on a day-to-day basis. However if you are 13 or 14 years old, think back to when you were 11 or 12 and how you have matured, how your interests have changed, and how you think about so many things in a different way than before.

4. Play video games in which the only way to beat the game is to make mistakes and learn from them. Many complex and challenging video games are built so that the games teach you how to play, but only through your mistakes. If you do not learn from your mistakes, you will not progress in the game. This type of willingness to adapt and change your approach is the core to being flexible.

Ask for Help

1. When you find yourself making the same mistakes time and time again it is an opportunity to recognize that you need to change your approach. This is a good time to ask others such as your friends or parents how they would approach the situation differently. Listen carefully and think about what you can do to solve the problem better.

2. Talk to someone who has already experienced the same situation. For example, if you are going on a trip to a foreign country you might want to talk to a friend or family member who has gone there so that you know what to expect and can be prepared to adapt. If you are involved in some type of complicated project such as putting together a model for a science fair or building something, you may wish to ask someone who has done it before to get hints and guidance about how that person approached the difficult task.

Helping Tools

1. Teach your parents about using their new cell phone or electronic device. Show them how you can take the device, making mistakes but also learning how to operate it by being creative and flexible in your approach. Find some frustrating and difficult apps or software that you do not initially understand and work through them, learning from your mistakes and recognizing that being flexible is the key to solving problems.

2. Get a book of brainteasers that require you to be very flexible in your thinking. Classic examples of simple brainteasers where a traditional way of approaching them will not solve the problem include *1000 PlayThinks* by Ivan Moscovich and *Entertain Your Brain* by Terry Stickels.

Chapter 9
Working Memory

If I Could Only Remember

Will was finishing up his first quarter in the ninth grade and was concerned about what his parents might say when they saw his report card. He was always an excellent student in elementary and middle school. However in ninth grade he began getting homework in every class and often forgot to complete assignments or write down all of his work. In the past his teachers usually wrote down homework assignments on the board and give him time to copy them down. Now, most of his teachers just told the class very quickly what was expected for the following day, and Will often had trouble remembering all of the details.

Will was also finding it much harder to learn everything that his teachers presented in class. Most of his teachers expected him to be able to listen to their lectures and take good notes at the same time. Will found it very difficult to do this, and as a result, his notes were incomplete and confusing, even to him.

Will was also confused about his difficulties with remembering what his teachers were saying. In fact he had a great memory. For example, he could tell you amazing details about his family's trip to the Grand Canyon and was able to remember all types of facts about his favorite football players. But remembering a few directions or keeping a thought in his mind for more than ten seconds was difficult for him.

This wasn't the first time that people had complained about his memory. His parents were always getting upset with him for being forgetful around the house. When they would tell him to do a few things at a time he would almost always forget to do one or two of them.

Will was experiencing some difficulties with his working memory. Working memory is very different from long-term memory, such as Will's knowledge about trips that he has taken and things that he has learned. Instead, it is a type of memory we use when we are trying to figure something out but need to do something with that information at the same time. Once Will learned that many of his problems were related to his difficulties with his working memory, he realized that there were a few things that he could do to improve himself.

The first thing that Will did was to make sure that he asked his teachers for clarification about his homework assignments when he wasn't able to keep them in mind long enough to write them down. The next thing he did was to begin spending more time listening in class rather than taking lengthy notes. He had asked a friend who was in most of his classes if he could copy his notes after class, freeing Will actively to listen to what the teacher was saying. This helped Will a great deal with his studying because he could focus his energy on listening, making it easier for him to learn. The last thing he did was to recognize that he was the type of person who needed to write things down to remember them. When his parents began to ask him to do some things around the house, he would stop them and make a list on his notepad that he had started to carry around with him. This helped him a lot at home, and his parents became very proud of him for being the one that they could count on to remember everything rather than to forget most of what they had just said.

▲▼▲▼▲▼▲▼▲▼

You really didn't need the skill of working memory too much when you were younger. Most of the time your parents and teachers were just telling you what to do or giving you simple instructions that were easy to follow. As you get older, people assume that you can do more; they expect you to remember a series of directions about doing your homework, keep in mind when a long term project is due, or remember all of the things that you need to pull together to go to your lacrosse practice or a field trip for school.

Many of the activities that teens are expected to do at home and in school require multiple steps like doing complex math problems in your head, remembering all of the things you need to do in a basketball play, or taking care of a series of chores at home. These tasks require working memory. Fortunately, there are a lot of things that you can do to compensate for poor working memory and to improve your working memory skills.

What is Working Memory?

Working memory involves the ability to remember something and to perform an activity while using this memory. It helps us to keep information in our mind so that we can use it for learning, figuring stuff out, or making things happen. Working memory involves both verbal and visual-spatial skills. Verbal working memory helps us to remember instructions and comprehend what we have heard. Visual-spatial working memory helps us to remember sequences of events and images and is important in math skills.

Some people confuse working memory with the term "short-term memory." While working memory does involve storing information temporarily, the difference is that working memory requires that you do something with that information. A good example of this might be when you are leaving your house and actively go to shut off your television, but at the same time have to remember to gather your coat, keys, and cell phone before leaving.

Working memory involves both the amount of information that you can store temporarily in your head and the length of time that you can keep it there. One interesting way to think about working memory is described by Dr. Tracy Packiam Alloway as "our brain's Post-It note."

Teenagers are typically able to remember between 4 and 6 instructions or ideas in their working memory. Interestingly, you actually reach your peak capacity for working memory between the ages of 16 and 35. When information is presented too quickly, a person with poor working memory may not have enough time to keep that information in mind and be able to process it.

If you have poor working memory skills you may have inherited them from your mother or father, and you might have to work really hard to improve. Fortunately, we now know some of the ways that you can improve your working memory and develop skills and strategies that help you support your working memory.

KNOW: *Where Do You Use Working Memory?*

Working memory is used in situations where you need to remember something at the same time that you are involved in an action. It helps you to make sure that you have remembered everything you need before leaving your house, that you take good notes during a class and perform multi-step directions. You need working memory to do math problems in your head, comprehend what you have read, and remember all of the rules of a game while you are playing it.

Working memory is helpful when you find yourself asking questions such as "What do I need to do next?" or "What was the homework assignment that my teacher just told us?" or "What is the sequence of events that happened on vacation?" When you find yourself asking these types of questions you need the skill of working memory.

Here is a list of common situations and activities that require working memory:

- Accurately writing down phone messages
- Remembering skills and strategies that have worked in the past and applying them to a new situation
- Following directions to get to a location
- Being able to explain the rules of a game to others
- Retelling a story in your own words in an organized, sequential manner
- Doing math in your head
- Following directions when putting something together
- Taking notes in the classroom
- Being able to remember the steps and ingredients necessary when cooking or following a recipe

Now that you **Know** a little more about where to use the skill of working memory, we will help you to see how using this skill helps you to do better in school, follow directions more accurately, and be more efficient at getting things done.

SHOW: *How It Helps*

Working memory skills will help you to do better at home and school because you will be able to follow more complicated directions. It will also help you improve the thinking skill of focus, because if you are able to keep more information in your mind you are less likely to get distracted by other things.

Improving your working memory will also help you to become less frustrated at home and school. Rather than getting to school and finding that you have forgotten to bring your homework or forgotten your lunch, you will know that you have everything with you. It will also make your parents and teachers happier with you, and you won't find them getting as angry with you for being forgetful.

Remember, earlier we told you that working memory was mostly inherited from your parents or other family members. This suggests that exercises and practice will improve it only so far. Truly improving working memory requires some tricks, knowledge, and strategies to reduce the requirements for using your working memory.

Think about this. If you use this strategy you won't have to remind yourself to take those things, simply look at the picture as a reminder. Of if someone asks you to do a math problem in your head such as "What is 7 times 8 plus 15?" the problem becomes much easier if you immediately have the knowledge that 7 times 8 = 56. Rather than keeping three pieces of information in mind you need to keep only two, and the problem becomes "What is 56 plus 15?"

GROW: *Using Working Memory in Daily Activities*

You can improve your ability to use working memory effectively by practicing some simple helping strategies and exercising your brain. You can improve your capacity for working memory by exercising your working memory through video games and other technologies.

Before you start developing strategies and exercising your working memory, decide what it is you want to improve. The following list will help you to set some clear and reachable goals. Check no more than two or three goals to work on at a time. It is difficult to work on too many at once, and one of the struggles for individuals with difficulties with working memory is their inability to do too many things at a time.

I want to improve my ability to:

_____ Remember more than the first or last things in a series of directions

_____ Organize my thoughts when I am telling a story or relating an experience

_____ Do math problems in my head

_____ Remember to bring everything to school

_____ Comprehend what I am reading

_____ Keep a sentence or thought in my mind long enough to remember it while writing

_____ Get better at taking notes in class

_____ Remember to take home or return forms such as permission slips and report cards

Help Yourself

1. Learn to chunk items by trying to remember two or more things as one item. You can learn to do this by repeatedly doing these activities together. For example, you can brush your teeth, wash your face, and comb your hair so that eventually these become one action that you perform in front of the mirror before school.

2. Repeat what you have heard such as a new name or a phone number in your a head a few times and at the same time add a visual image in your head of what you are thinking about. For example, if you meet a new person you might say Sammy Smith with brown eyes while picturing an image of Sammy in your head.

3. Recognize your need for devices to enhance your working memory skills. Just as an individual with vision issues requires glasses or may need to sit in the front of the class, individuals with working memory difficulties often need devices or accommodations to help them. Once you become truly aware of this, you can take active steps to reduce difficulties caused by working memory problems. Recognize that you need to ask the teacher to repeat directions when you cannot remember them. You may need

to work very hard to focus on what people are saying, particularly when they are giving you homework, directions about something to do, or relating important information to you. You also need to have other methods for recording information, whether it be taking pictures with your cell phone; always having an agenda, notepad, and pen in your pocket; or sending yourself text or voice reminders of what you need to do later.

4. Exercise your working memory by exercising your body and stretching your brain's capacity. There is evidence indicating that physical exercise can improve memory and help to improve attention. You might want to think about exercising before studying for an important test.

Ask for Help

1. If you struggle with working memory, you can remember only a few things at a time. Sometimes you will simply need to ask people to repeat what they have said to you. When you are asking people to repeat something, it is imperative that you explain to them that you are trying to listen and follow what they are saying but are struggling to remember one or two things. If you show them that you remember part of what they have said but need them to explain the rest, they are more likely to repeat themselves and not feel that you weren't trying. In addition, if you write down what they are saying they will realize how serious you are about trying to remember what you have been told.

2. Ask to borrow your friend's notes from class. Many individuals with working memory difficulties tend to struggle when taking notes. Note taking requires the ability to hold many pieces of information in your mind. You must be able to take verbal directions that may be presented very quickly and you also must process all of that information while you are writing.

This is a frequent complaint of high school and college students who have memory difficulties. If this happens to you, talk to your teacher about this difficulty or borrow notes from a friend. We recommend that instead of trying to write down everything that your teacher says while in class, try to put down just the main ideas and leave room for lists in between these ideas. Later you will be able to copy your friend's notes into these areas, and perhaps learning will come easier to you because you are spending your time listening rather than attempting to write.

Helping Tools

1. It is useful to exercise your mind by stretching your working memory. Some simple strategies include playing memory board games or doing memory exercises in your head. For example, you might want to try to remember all 50 states or list all of the former presidents or something else that may be of interest to you.

   There is some excellent scientific research that indicates that computer programs such as Cogmed Working Memory Training can improve your working memory skills. You might also try to use computer and video games that require sustaining memory.

2. Eat memory foods. While there is not any one food that has been demonstrated to improve your memory in and of itself, there is increasing evidence that what you eat can increase both focus and memory. There is some evidence that Omega-3 fatty acids found in foods such as salmon and tuna may be helpful to improve attention and focus. Protein is also described as brain food. Sources of protein including soy, poultry, and protein bars. There is also evidence that magnesium, which is contained in nuts and dark leafy vegetables such as spinach, can be helpful, as well. Interestingly, all of these suggestions of specific foods are quite healthy and are uniformly seen as being good for you, which is likely to add to your overall physical wellbeing.

Chapter 10
Self Awareness

I Understand, I Understand

Zach was almost 13 years old when he started in his sixth grade classroom at a new middle school. He had just moved into the area from a nearby town and didn't know anybody well at his new school. In his old school he had a couple of friends that he had known since preschool. His old friends always thought that Zach was a little different, but they knew he was a really great friend.

When Zach got to the new middle school he was so anxious about making new friends that he scared off some kids. He would introduce himself to the kids and start talking about all of the things that he liked to do, and some of the new kids thought that he was strange and did not want to spend much time with him. Zach wasn't doing much listening in these conversations. He was so concerned about making friends that he seemed to rush into activities and didn't spend much time figuring out what the other kids were interested in or what they were talking about.

After a few weeks of school Zach came home and told his parents that he hated his new school and that he wanted to move back to be with his old friends. He became very upset and told his parents that the other kids would not talk to him, no one invited him to sit with them at lunchtime, and no one had chosen to work with him on the science project earlier that day. His parents asked him how he was going about trying to make new friends, and they realized that Zach was being overly enthusiastic with the other kids and maybe scaring them off. As they listened to Zach talk about his difficulties, they asked him to tell them something about the kids that he was trying to be friends with, and it became evident that Zach didn't know much about them.

Zach's inability to understand his feelings and the feelings and thoughts of his classmates was interfering with his ability to make friends at his new school. Once Zach's parents talked to him about it, they helped him to see that he was trying too hard to make friends. It was almost as if the other kids were picking up on the fact that Zach was obsessed with making new friends, and they wanted nothing to do with him.

In addition, Zach's parents talked to him about trying to understand what interested the other kids and helped Zach become more in tune with their interests. Zach's parents worked with him to improve his listening skills so that he could learn about what the other kids were doing and quietly join in with them.

Zach found a few other kids that he thought he could be friends with and joined the computer and videogame club that met after school. He used it as an opportunity to ask other club members what games they were playing at home and what they liked best. This was the start of Zach making some friends at school, and soon he had a group of buddies to eat lunch with and hang out with after school.

▲▼▲▼▲▼▲▼▲▼

It seems that as you move from middle to high school, peer relationships become increasingly important. They also become more complicated, with far more drama. In addition, there is probably a lot more going on in your own head, as you are trying to figure out stuff about yourself, your own feelings, and your relationships with others.

You need the skills of self-awareness to help you to look at your own way of thinking about things as well the skills that help you to understand others. Some people seem to be naturally good at these skills. They seem to get along with everybody and always appear to be comfortable with who they are. Others need to work at it; they need to work hard to figure out what is making them feel the way they do or to tune into what is going on with other people.

What is Self Awareness?

Self-awareness is a thinking skill that helps you to judge your actions and to respond appropriately to social situations. It helps you to know if you are talking too loudly in the library when other children are trying to work, to know your strengths and weaknesses, and to pick up on important social cues in your interactions with others.

Self-awareness is a skill that helps you to know what and when to do something. By understanding yourself and others, you can more easily solve problems, resolve conflicts, and improve your relationships with others. Developing self-awareness skills does not help with every relationship that you will have. You are very likely to struggle to get along with some difficult teachers and peers in your world. You might even have people in your family that you get along with better than others or those who you just can't seem to understand. However by working on your understanding of yourself, you are likely to develop the skill that will help you to know what makes you happy and to engage in the actions and behaviors to get there.

KNOW: *Where Do You Use Self Awareness?*

You use self-awareness when you describe yourself accurately. Good self-awareness skills are used when you are able to recognize when you have made a mistake, take responsibility for it, and learn from it. Self-awareness helps you to know how much to study for a test, make accurate predictions about the impact of your behavior upon others, and estimate your grades and performance on tests and quizzes.

Self-awareness skills are also seen in your accuracy in understanding other people's behavior and emotions. They are the skills you use when you attempt to make a decision about how to approach another person or when you have had a conflict with someone else.

Self awareness is helpful when you find yourself asking, "How do I really feel about this?" or "What's making me feel so angry?" or "Why is everybody ignoring me?"

Here is a list of common situations and activities that require self awareness:

- Working on school project with other students in your class

- Estimating how well you did on a recent test or quiz

- Being able accurately to describe your feelings about another person

- Checking over your test before handing it in to the teacher

- Making a decision about something and explaining why you made that decision

- Being caring when one of your friends has experienced a death in the family

- Recognizing when one of your friends is feeling lonely or depressed

Now that you **Know** a little more about where to use the skill of working memory, we will help you to see how using this skill helps you to do better in school, follow directions more accurately, and be more efficient at getting things done.

SHOW: *How It Helps*

Self-awareness allows you to be a better judge of yourself and others. It assists you in your performance at school because good self-awareness skills are a part of checking on schoolwork and recognizing how much studying you need to do in order to perform well on a test.

Self-awareness skills also help you in navigating the confusion of relationships with teenage peers. Good self-awareness skills help you to know when there is something that you really should feel upset about and when you should ignore certain situations. It won't help you to get along with everyone because you cannot control how others feel, but it will help you know how to be caring and understanding of others and be a good friend.

GROW: *Using Self-awareness in Daily Activities*

Self-awareness is a skill that usually develops over time. It is not something that you can decide that you want to get better at today and be there tomorrow. Because people are very complex, it takes a great deal of thinking and awareness truly to understand yourself and others. Just when you think you've got it, there's more to learn.

Before you start practicing your self-awareness skills, it is best to decide the areas that you would like to improve. The following list will help you to set clear and reachable goals. Check no more than two or three goals to work on at a time. Use your self-awareness skills to figure out which are the most important skills for you to work on presently.

I want to improve my ability to:

_____ Make friends

_____ Joke around appropriately with my friends and teachers

_____ Say "I'm sorry" when I do something wrong

_____ Recognize my strengths and weaknesses

_____ Accurately estimate my performance on a test or quiz

_____ Recognize how much I need to study before a test

_____ Check over my work more regularly before I turn it in

_____ Work cooperatively with others on school projects

Help Yourself

1. To improve your ability to accurately see your personal strengths and weaknesses, make a list. Then ask someone who knows you well—such as a good friend or a parent—to do the same so that you can compare lists and talk about where there are differences.

2. Practice your listening skills. In order to do this you need to allow other people to speak without interrupting, pay attention to not only what they are saying but also how they are saying it, and what their body is telling you. Check the accuracy about what you have understood by paraphrasing what has been said to you, starting your sentences with "What I hear you saying is" or "It sounds like." Don't simply mimic what they have said when paraphrasing but really try to understand their thoughts and feelings.

3. Get in the habit of checking over your schoolwork and performance in chores. While it is not healthy to obsess about these issues or to become overly concerned about being perfect, many teens who struggle with self-awareness do not spend enough time looking over their work, making corrections to silly errors, or giving themselves an opportunity to re-think what they may have written.

4. Spoil your friends and your family. Do what they want. By this, we are suggesting that you think about other people's likes and desires rather than your own. For example, when you have a friend over, think about playing a game or engaging in an activity that they enjoy rather than just doing what you want to do. With your family, think about what you can do to be helpful to them and work on giving back some of the love that you receive from your parents.

5. Hone your predictive skills. Try to estimate the outcome of a situation. For example, think about the different factors and obstacles that might affect the success of a task such as a science project, soccer game, or musical performance. Keep track of your predictions in a journal and make comments about the factors that influence the accuracy of your predictions.

Ask for Help

1. Talk to your parents about some of your household rules and expectations and discuss the possibility of changing them. Do this without confrontation and more as an exercise to reflect on the reasoning behind them. For example, if your parents have strict rules for bedtime or the use of technology, discuss their thinking about this, show them that you are listening to their rationale, and if you have suggestions for modest changes, show them that you can be reasonable in your discussion with them.

2. Get together with some of your friends who may be more socially active than you. This may help you in increasing the number of friends that you have and improving your social skills. When a friend is introducing you to some new kids, make it a point to find out about their interests and what you have in common.

Helping Tools

1. If you really want to see what you are like, ask someone to take video of you in real life. This often works best when someone is taking video of your entire family or you and a bunch of friends, rather than focusing on you. You will get a chance to see some of your mannerisms with other people, listen to your voice on tape, and get a better sense of how you might appear to others.

2. Play a massive online multi-player roleplaying game. Online games such as World of Warcraft, Lord of the Rings, and League of Legends are games where you need to work with guilds or teams of other players and learn to adapt to new situations when there is a new set of rules and expectations.

Chapter 11
High-tech Ways to Improve Your Skills

Mom, Dad, I Need My Cell Phone!

If you are struggling with your executive functions and your birth date was in the 1990s or 2000s, you are a very lucky person. First of all, we know a lot more about how difficulties in executive functions can affect you. So instead of getting into trouble for being disorganized or being punished for losing your focus, you might find your parents, educators, and doctors are better able to understand you and can help you work on improving these skills.

You are also lucky to have been born in a time when so many technologies are available that can either directly improve your executive functioning skills or serve as a tool that you can use to improve your executive functions. Some technologies such as online working memory training programs, video games that can improve focus and processing speed skills, and brain-training programs that can improve flexibility show promise in their ability to make changes in the structure of your brain and how it works. Other technologies such as cell phones that help you to be more organized, digital cameras that can reduce the strain of using your working memory by helping you to remember, and computer software that can assist you with your planning and self-awareness are incredibly powerful tools for people who struggle with executive functions.

Just as the invention of eyeglasses transformed the world because poor vision was no longer an obstacle for success, technologies can make the world a different place for people with executive functioning difficulties. However, just like glasses, you need to put them on and then do the work so that they can allow you to see. Digital technologies are only as good as your decisions about when and how to use them. Having a cell phone won't keep you any better organized, assist you in planning, or improve your time management if you don't decide to use it as a tool to help you.

In each of the previous chapters we have given you a few ideas about technological tools that could be helpful in improving many executive functions. This chapter will provide you with a few more ideas. Again, we want to stress that it isn't the tools themselves, but how you use them to support, practice, and master executive functions skills that will make a difference in your executive function skills.

To help you use this section, we have chosen to describe some of the executive skills that you can work on improving with popular technologies. One way to use this section is to look at the technologies that you use most often and explore some of the executive functions that they might help you improve.

Search Engines

Do you ever use a search engine like Google, Bing, or Yahoo to look up something or learn about something new? There are not too many kids who can answer "no" to that question. When you use a search engine have you ever thought that you are using all different types of executive functioning skills to do it effectively? Probably not. Believe it or not, simply by thinking about executive functions and becoming more aware of what you are doing may improve some of these skills.

For starters, you use the executive functioning skill of planning when using search engines by choosing key words to use in a search. Doing an advanced search where you combine words or use modifiers like quotation marks requires that you use your planning skills to get to the end result of your search. Flexibility is another executive function skill that is needed for doing an Internet search. Your first search doesn't always produce the results you were looking for, so you need to adapt by changing the key words. You can often learn a lot about what you need to change by exploring the results of an initial search. You might also choose to use a different search engine and see if that produces better results. All of these approaches require good flexibility skills. Focusing skills are also important when doing an Internet search, because it is easy to get distracted by reading and learning about something new that wasn't a part of your original reason for searching. When you are scanning the results of a search you need to be able to do it quickly and not get distracted by material that doesn't apply to your current work. So, as you can see, there are many ways to use something that you are already accustomed to doing, such as an Internet search, for strengthening your executive function skills.

iPods and Media Players

When the original iPod and Mp3 players were introduced, they were basically places to store music and listen to it easily. Current versions of media players allow you to organize all media files including movies, music, television shows, and videos. Most of them now allow you to play games, take video, download apps, check your email, and store your pictures. Who knows what the next generation of media players will do. Because media players have so many functions, they also support many different executive functions.

These include:

Organization: When you import music into your Mp3 player you can organize it in many different ways, including grouping music into different genres, by band, or by creating your own play lists.

Planning: Creating playlists requires thinking ahead and often involves some revisions. For example, you might choose to create a playlist for a birthday party that includes some of your friend's favorite music.

Focus: Many kids who have difficulties paying attention or sustaining their effort when doing homework may find that they do better when listening to music. Try finding the music that works best for you and use it on a regular basis. Music can also be very useful for encouraging you when you are doing something difficult. You probably notice that many people use iPods when they are running or exercising in the gym, as this may help to keep up their energy. In the same way, many kids report that it is helpful to have loud music playing when they are doing chores that they dislike because it helps them to focus and block out the unpleasant aspects of the situation.

Cell Phones

If you are like most teenagers, your cell phone is probably one of your most important possessions. While many of you have probably misplaced your cell phone a few times, it is amazing how rarely kids actually lose their cell phones, because their cell phone is so important to them. In today's world a cell phone allows you to communicate and be in contact with your friends and family instantly at any time of the day or night, and texting has made communicating even more convenient.

In addition to being a great way to communicate and stay in touch with important people in your life, cell phones are also great tools for helping kids who have difficulties with executive functions. Today's smartphones can sometimes make up for some of the difficulties that you may be having with your own executive function through the use of alarms, built-in cameras, and voice recorders. For example, cell phones can help you with organization by allowing you to create contact lists with your phone numbers. You might choose to organize some of your friends by the classes that they are in so that you know whom to call if you happen to forget your homework or don't know an assignment. Cell phones can also help you will self-awareness skills by allowing you to keep in contact with your friends and know what's going on with them. Texting or calling your friends helps you to be aware of how they are feeling and what is going on in their lives, and in turn also can help you to become a better friend. Also, personalizing your phone such as using customized ringtones helps you to understand a little bit more about who you are as a person and helps you to display that personality to others.

Blogging

Blogging is a great way to share information about something you think is important. In addition to practicing your writing skills and sharing your opinions, you can help other people learn about a subject of importance. Creating a blog can help you identify and expand a sense of understanding of yourself. Blogging is also a great help to some of your academic skills and interests because having a good blog involves research and attention to your writing skills.

Self awareness: Blogs are great for helping you to share what is important to you with other people. It is important that as you write the blog, you have an understanding of what other people will be interested in reading. Otherwise, no one will read it. You also need to be careful about not being offensive and driving away readers.

A well-informed blog is also written in a way to encourage readers to leave their comments. Self-awareness becomes important in writing about content that will inspire others to respond to you.

Organization: By definition, blogging requires good writing skills. If you want people to read your blog you must write in an organized, logical fashion. Good blogs often have follow-ups to comments or previous posts, which involves organizational skills so that you do not repeat yourself.

Social Networks

Social networks may be the most popular way that teenagers use the Internet today. While many teenagers think that social networks means Facebook, there are other social networks, as well. There are also sites for younger kids and preteens, as well as a number of social networks that focus around games or other areas of interest. Executive functions used on Facebook and other social networks play a role in what you share about yourself, how you organize material about yourself, and how you react to what others may post.

Organization: You will want to organize information about yourself and put it together in an interesting way. You may want to share information about a recent trip or an event. You might want to think about how you organize your pictures and the text that go along with them.

Self-awareness: Issues of privacy are very important in social networks. You need to think about what it is that you want people to know about you. Consideration of other people's feelings, while not face-to-face, is very important. Something like ignoring a friend's request can hurt the feelings of others and may cause some tensions in your relationships. Thinking about the types of pictures that you post about yourself is also important to consider. It is one thing to show your best friend a picture or something that might be embarrassing, another thing to post it on Facebook, where it becomes available for others to see.

Self-control: There will be times when you see something posted that may anger you. Learning to stop before you type in a response is a very important skill for social networking. Once you send it out, it is very difficult to take back.

Brain Training and Cognitive Fitness Tools

A number of brain training websites and other technologies have shown promise in directly helping with executive functioning skills. These include tools such as biofeedback and neurofeedback, which can improve focusing skills, and websites such as happyneuron.com that have games designed to improve executive function skills. Working memory training (Cogmed.com) is a memory training program that helps many students improve their focus, working memory, and academic skills. Because each of these programs has different approaches, they may work more for one particular skill than for another.

Working memory: Many of the cognitive fitness programs have specific games or programs to improve working memory. These programs strengthen your working memory by increasing how much and how long you can remember verbal and visual materials. These programs work well as long as you put in the time, effort, and practice.

Focus: There are many cognitive fitness programs to improve how long you can sustain your focus. Some of the programs also help you to develop selective attention skills so that you are able to shift your focus effectively from one thing to another and not because you are distracted.

Flexibility: Many cognitive training programs improve flexibility by helping your brain to shift from one thing to another more quickly and accurately. This can be particularly helpful in improving your problem solving skills.

As newer and more sophisticated technologies are developed, there will be many other ways that technology can serve to support, practice, and help you master executive functioning skills. Fortunately, educators and psychologists are becoming more aware about how digital technologies help kids in developing executive functioning skills. But a lot of times kids actually know more about the newest technologies than adults do. If you find a new tool or technology that helps you stay more organized or improves your focus, share it with your friends and teachers. You will be using your executive skills while helping others.

Chapter 12
Keep on Going and Growing

You Will Get Better and Better

Many of you who are reading this book have chosen to do so because you, your parents, or your teachers have noticed your difficulty in solving problems, paying attention, and working to your potential. We hope you've learned that many of these difficulties can be a result of problems in using your executive-functioning skills. As we described, these skills start as brain-based capacities, so you may have a weakness in one or more areas of your executive functions. However, that's not the end of the story. Because of the latest research in neuroscience, we now know that you can improve these executive functions through training, practice, and strategies.

Prior to 2001 most psychologists and neuroscientists believed that the physical structure and capacities of your brain could not change after the first few years of life. Scientists believed that mental capacities such as memory, focus, and processing of information were a result of genetics and your earliest experiences as an infant and young child. The belief was that you were essentially stuck with your brain as it was and that there was nothing that could be done to grow and improve your brain. In the last 10 or so years, sophisticated ways of imaging the brain have revealed that brain exercises, activities, and experience can actually change the wiring and biochemistry of the brain. Reshaping and growing the brain is called neuroplasticity, and it is one of the key ingredients to what you have done in this book.

This book has hundreds of suggestions about things you can do to improve your executive functions that also lead to improvement in academic skills. To do so you need to be able to identify the skills you want to improve and then systematically go about doing so. We want to remind you of a few of the key ingredients that will make your efforts a success.

First of all, we now know from a wealth of scientific research that training and practice not only improve your skills, but also change your brain and build its capacity to use these skills. Just as repeated practice of an instrument changes the structure of your brain, repeated practice of these executive skills will change the connections and biochemistry of your brain.

Secondly, having a growth mindset that encourages you to keep working on these skills will help you to build them. In part, a growth mindset will encourage sustained practice. More than that, it helps you to have the confidence that your practice will bring improvements to many parts of your life.

Thirdly, even with skills you think you'll never become particularly good at, there are lots of tools and strategies that can help you to compensate for an area of weakness. For example, if you're not the most organized person in the world and don't want to devote too much of your energy to becoming that person, you can still find ways to make things easier on yourself. You can use some of the tools and technologies that we've described to help you with organization. Select a few priority areas for yourself where you want to be organized and focus on those. As you move into adulthood, pair yourself with roommates, friends, a spouse, or fellow workers who take on some of the responsibilities of organization while you contribute in another way.

Lastly, while this is a book about improving your skills, it's perfectly fine if you do not excel in all of these areas. Improving your skills to the point where they do not cause serious hardship or hold you back from achieving your goals is the key. Beyond that, we strongly encourage you to look at those areas in your life where your skills and interests are a good fit, where you get excited about what you are doing, and where you are able to apply your executive skills in an efficient and productive manner.

We think that kids (and adults) are happiest when their skills are a good match for the demands of their work and relationships. For example, if you are a very outgoing, friendly person, we want to encourage you to think about your life's work as something that involves doing things with other people. If you're someone who loves the outdoors and feels alive, focused, and engaged when you're doing something outside, don't work in a cubicle on the 40th floor of a skyscraper. If you find that you are most focused when surfing the Internet or playing a video game, think about getting a job in the technology field.

We encourage you to become more aware of your strengths and weaknesses. We all have them, and by having more insight into your makeup, you become more capable of understanding problems and coming up with good solutions for them. However as we've said throughout every chapter of this book, awareness is only the beginning. If you practice the skills you want to improve, you will get better at using them. And using them well will help you to get things done, feel better about yourself, and just be happier.

Addendum: Parents' Guide

Note to Parents and Educators

Most children with executive-functioning difficulties come by them naturally. That is to say, their parents might have had similar difficulties. Recent studies suggest that 90% of executive-functioning difficulties may be inherited. This would suggest that many parents of children who struggle with issues such as organization, time management, and working memory will experience the same difficulties themselves. Many of these adults have developed their own personal strategies for these executive dysfunctions. They may keep lists; use sticky pads for reminders; develop routines that they can remember; or rely upon a spouse, partner, or secretary to compensate for their difficulties.

Many children do not intuitively develop and learn executive skills. Just because these skills are not acquired easily by simple observation or repetition does not mean that these children cannot become quite adept at executive skills. It does mean, however, that parents, educators, and at times even older siblings and peers can play a very powerful role in helping these children develop their executive skills.

Children and teens who strive to acquire executive skills often have difficulty in generalizing or applying their knowledge from one situation to another. For example, they may be very interested in organizing their playlists for an iPod or their contacts on their cell phones, but have difficulty naturally applying these same skills to having their homework organized. Children and teens often do better when they are helped to apply executive skills at the "point of performance." In other words, if we can help them identify executive skills that they are already using and then show them how to practice these skills in the place that they need to use them, they are more likely to be successful.

How to teach executive functions

1. **Develop a partnership**—Talk with your children about their experiences or difficulties with specific executive skills. For example, it would be helpful to speak to children who have difficulties in regulating emotions to get them to express an interest in learning how to be less irritable and not to get angry as easily. To the degree that this becomes a shared goal rather than a parent's or teacher's desire, children are likely to participate in efforts towards improvement.

2. **Make the learning goals explicit**—Once you have a partnership with your child you can begin working on developing very clear goals as to what you want to change and how you want to improve it. Rather than simply saying, "We want you to be a more flexible person," it is far better to set specific goals within the broader context. For example, while you might say to your child, "We'd like you to become more flexible so that we could go to more places as a family," it often works better to say, "We would like you to try more foods so the family can go to some other restaurants." At that point, you may want to work with the child to find other foods or restaurants the child might be willing to try. Rather than stating, "We want you to become more organized," pick one or two areas on which to focus. For example, having the goal of keeping a backpack organized so that homework does not get lost is clear and may be easier to change than having a bedroom be organized.

3. **Preview strategies** that help children understand when they are using and need executive skills—Many times children use executive skills without recognizing that they have done so. This is quite common in video games, where children frequently need to organize, plan, and manage their time to "beat a level." Help children to recognize when a particular skill will be needed by previewing a situation before they enter it. For example, children who have difficulty with the executive skill of focusing while getting started on homework or chores are likely to benefit from a brief discussion with their parents that help them consider where they should start and exactly what they should do. Many children with executive dysfunctions benefit from an expansive form of previewing. For example, rather than saying, "Tomorrow morning we need to get up early for school," it may be helpful to describe exactly what time they would need to get up and why the family is getting up early, and jointly to develop strategies that will assist them in being prepared.

4. **Metacognition** refers to thinking about one's thought. It is the ability to be reflective and step back and self-observe. It is an important skill to teach children with executive dysfunctions because they often have significant problems in this capacity. For example, many children with metacognitive difficulties do not check their schoolwork, are unable to describe their reasoning for decision making, and have difficulty in understanding how well they have completed a task.

Parents and teachers play a significant role in facilitating metacognitive strategies. A number of approaches may be helpful. These include asking children to estimate how they have done on a test at school or a chore at home, engaging in a discussion about the strategies that they have used to be successful in a video game, or developing a chart that accurately describes their strengths and weaknesses. Parents and teachers can also model metacognitive strategies. They can talk out loud about their strategies for solving a problem, make comments about how they have learned from mistakes, and check their spelling or other work on an e-mail or in communication with others.

5. **Practicing executive skills** in an interesting and reinforcing manner—To the degree that parents and educators can make the practice and development of executive skills fun and stimulating, children are more likely to engage in them. This could be as simple as playing children's favorite music when they are emptying out and organizing their backpacks on a weekly basis to developing family-competition strategies (in which there is no loser) to help them become more efficient in completing chores or homework. The use of many types of digital technologies, including video games, can be very helpful in practicing and developing executive skills. However as with any type of practice of executive skills that are not directly related to the task, parents, educators, and others need to help children make the connection from the fun practice of executive skills to a real-world practice of skills.

6. **Recognizing a child's improved use of executive skills**—This is a key ingredient to ongoing success. It helps children to identify an executive skill that they are using effectively. Then, they can more readily see how their efforts and practice have resulted in improvement. Helping children to see that "practice makes perfect" provides both recognition and the impetus to apply these executive skills in other areas.

7. **Generalization of executive skills** to the real world—Generalization refers to effectively applying a strategy that is learned in one setting to another setting. For example, children may learn the skill of self-control in the classroom, such as when they keep their hands to themselves and don't interrupt others, but have a hard time applying those same skills on the playground or in an after-school setting.

In order to assist in generalization, it is important to identify where the executive skills may be useful at home and school. Point out to your children how a particular skill, for example, focus will help them become better athletes or musicians. Next, reinforce the use of this executive skill across many settings through verbal praise, rewards, and privileges. Children who have difficulties in these areas often do not recognize that the same skills may help them in many different situations. For example, the metacognitive skill of estimation may help children recognize their strengths and weaknesses in a sport, an academic subject, or as an artist.

Encouraging children to practice their newly-acquired executive skills across settings will be helpful. Generalization is enhanced when children are able to identify on their own when they are using an executive skill. Having other instructors besides parents and teachers such as grandparents, older siblings, or friends recognize and reinforce the use of executive skills in situations is also very helpful. Teach children to ask for help when applying executive skills in new settings, as well.

8. **Maintaining executive skills** or other behaviors requires consistent reinforcement, recognition, and success—Helping children continually to see how these executive skills are helping them in accomplishing tasks such as homework and chores will be useful. Rewards and reinforcement such as verbal praise, privileges based upon accomplishment and effort, and recognition by peers or teachers can be very powerful in maintaining the use of executive skills across areas. At some point, teaching children to provide their own reinforcement by recognizing their successful use of executive skills is indicated.

More information about executive functions

Executive functions are brain-based cognitive skills involving critical thinking and self-regulation. They impact goal setting, problem solving, and decision making. They include a set of related skills that help prioritize, regulate, and orchestrate an individual's thoughts and behaviors. Executive functions help individuals manage their feelings and actions, monitor their behaviors, and attend to their experiences from the past and the present.

There are dozens of definitions for executive functions. Further information about executive functions can be found in references for Russell Barkley (2006), Thomas Brown (2005), and Peg Dawson and Richard Guare (2009, 2010). The model used in *Train Your Brain for Success* is a modification of definitions described by Peg Dawson and Richard Guare. Their descriptions are an excellent fit for understanding how children use executive functions in their day-to-day lives.

It is important to emphasize that the executive skills described in this definition are often connected or interdependent and that many examples of executive dysfunctions, such as problems in completing homework, may involve a range of executive-function skills such as time management, perseverance, organization, and sustained attention.

How do I know if my child has difficulties with executive functions?

While many children who have severe difficulties with executive dysfunctions have a psychiatric diagnosis such as Attention Deficit/Hyperactivity Disorder, Learning Disability, Asperger's Disorder, Anxiety Disorder, Depression, or an Autistic Spectrum Disorder, there are also many children who display more moderate executive-skills difficulties. These children may have specific areas of weakness such as problems with social thinking or more general concerns such as difficulties with sustaining their attention and effort to tasks.

Parents are encouraged to educate themselves about executive functions. A few web-based resources, including Learningworksforkids.com, are noted at the end of this section. When these problems are significantly impacting your child's performance, parents are encouraged to obtain a psychological evaluation that includes cognitive, neuro-psychological, and educational testing.

A parent's guide to the 8 executive functions

Organization

- Systematic approach to facilitate goal-directed behavior.
- Sequencing, analysis of a complex situation, and arranging elements into a functioning whole.
- Promotes efficiency, task completion, and creating a unified approach to a task.

Planning

- Development of a road map or set of strategies to accomplish a goal.
- Encompasses both short- and long-term goals and a clear sense of environmental and social cues.
- Estimation, anticipation of outcomes, and use of previous experiences are often important components of planning.

Focus

- The capacity to maintain one's focus and attention in the presence of distractions and other activities.
- Assists individuals in being able selectively to choose what is most important when a series of stimuli needs to be attended to.
- Understanding what is expected in a task and having the skills to direct one's attention from one task to another.

Time management

- The capacity to complete tasks in a timely and efficient fashion.
- Required to make and follow a schedule.
- Accurate estimation skills and the capacity to monitor one's effort and actions and have an appropriate sense of urgency for completing tasks.

Self-Control

- The capacity to manage one's feeling effectively, to handle frustration or teasing.

- Understanding one's feelings and expressing oneself in an appropriate fashion.

- Emotional self-control that allows an individual to handle difficult situations.

- Behavioral self-control, helps an individual not to engage in impulsive behavior.

- Facilitates the ability to delay gratification and use reflective, rather than reactive, behaviors to situations.

Flexibility

- The capacity to improvise, shift approaches, and be adaptable to the demands of the situation.

- Recognition of the need to utilize different problem-solving strategies, including reflective, careful approaches, or a trial-and-error/random approach.

Working Memory

- The capacity to keep things in mind while actively being engaged in an activity on these things.

- A core component in the ability to follow multi-step directions, complete mathematical calculations in one's head, and many problem-solving activities.

- Important role in reading and other academic skills.

Self-Awareness

- Self-monitoring and self-observation.

- Helps children check on their successes and failures and gain perspective on their decision making.

- Involves the ability to label and describe one's feelings and to understand the feelings and expressions of others.

- The capacity to read and understand nonverbal cues, understand social conventions, and express care and compassion towards others.

Additional References for Parents

Barkley, R. (2006). *Attention-Deficit Hyperactivity Disorder, Third Edition: A Handbook for Diagnosis and Treatment.* New York, NY: Guilford Press.

Bronson, P., & Merryman, A. (2009). *Nurture Shock: New Thinking About Children.* New York, NY: Twelve Publishing.

Brown, T. (2005). *Attention Deficit Disorder: The Unfocused Mind in Children and Adults.* New Haven, CT: Yale University Press.

Dawson, P. & Guare, R. (2010). *Executive Skills in Children and Adolescents, Second Edition: A Practical Guide to Assessment and Intervention* (The Guilford Practical Intervention in Schools Series). New York, NY: Guilford Press.

Dawson, P. & Guare, R. (2009). *Smart but Scattered: The Revolutionary "Executive Skills" Approach to Helping Kids Reach Their Potential.* New York, NY: Guilford Press.

Galinsky, E. (2010). *Mind in the Making: The Seven Essential Life Skills Every Child Needs.* Harper Paperbacks.

Kaufman, C. (2010). *Executive Function in the Classroom: Practical Strategies for Improving Performance and Enhancing Skills for All Students.* Baltimore, MD: Paul H. Brookes Publishing.

Klingberg, T. (2009). *The Overflowing Brain: Information Overload and the Limits of Working Memory.* New York, NY: Oxford University Press.

Kutscher, M.L. & Moran, M. (2009). *Organizing the Disorganized Child: Simple Strategies to Succeed in School.* New York, NY: Harper Studio.

Meltzer, L. (Ed). (2010). *Executive Function in Education: From Theory to Practice.* New York, NY: Guilford Press.

Meltzer, L. (2010). *Promoting Executive Function in the Classroom (What Works for Special-Needs Learners).* New York, NY: Guilford Press.